Principles of Belief and Practices of Faith

A Guide to Successful Living
Volume I

Dr. Beresford Adams

Bee and Gee Publishers, LLC
Coram, NY
www.beeandgeepublishers.com

ISBN 1-4392-2151-0

Dedication

I dedicate this book to my wife and best friend
Dr. Gloria Elena Maxwell Adams.

CONTENTS

Dr. Beresford Adams is the senior pastor of Faith Baptist Church of Coram, New York. He lectures and conducts seminars nationally and internationally on human relationships, wholesome living, faith crises management, faith growth, and spirituality.

Dr. Adams is a graduate of Princeton Theological Seminary and Drew University.

Principles of Belief and Practices of Faith

A Guide to Successful Living
Volume I

INTRODUCTION

Now faith is the substance of things hoped for, the evidence of things not seen. Hebrews 11:1

PRINCIPLES

Principles can be defined in several ways. They are laws that govern the processes of events. They are truths that determine the results of occurrences. In addition, principles can be described as rules or standards influencing the consequences of good and bad behaviors.

The Bible contains laws, truths, and standards relating to people's conduct. Therefore, there are many principles in the Bible. There are some biblical principles that I choose to call principles of belief.

BELIEF

We often use the word belief not to express confidence but to state uncertainties. For instance, usually we are expressing a feeling or notion when we say, "I believe that it might rain tomorrow." We certainly don't mean that we are sure that it will rain. However, we shouldn't use the word belief in this sense regarding our relationship to God. It is better to use the word belief to declare definite truths about God. For example, when we say, "I believe that God exists," we should mean that we are confident that God lives. Hebrews 11: 6 states, "…for the person who comes to God must believe that He is." Belief in this sense is to be positive of a truth without proof. In matters concerning God, this is always the case.

With respect to biblical principles, it is not just what we believe but how we believe. For instance, if we believe in God, are we willing to follow the principles He gives us? We should believe in biblical principles because they are God's blueprints by which we can build our lives. Furthermore, principles in the Bible out-line clear objectives and goals that God has for our lives. In this regard, principles of belief are about making the right choices-God's choices for us.

• Belief and Faith

Belief and faith are often used interchange-ably in our everyday speech. However, for a better understanding of biblical principles of belief, I suggest that we consider belief and faith in the Bible as separate things. Belief in the Bible is in effect related to people's per-ception of God's power to intervene in human events. Faith in the Bible, for all intents and purposes, always pointed to the mighty acts of God or the powerful acts of people by the might of God.

The fact that people are capable of hav-ing extraordinary powers through God is indicated in what Jesus said to his disciples af-ter an incident recorded in verses 14 through 18 of the seventh chapter of Matthew. A man brought his sick son to some of Jesus' disciples. The disciples tried but couldn't heal him. Then the man took his son to Jesus. Jesus promptly healed him. After this, Matthew recorded the following:

> *Then, the disciples came to Jesus when He was by Himself and they asked Him, "Why could we not heal him?" Jesus answered them, "Because of your <u>unbelief;</u> for truthfully I tell you, if you have <u>faith</u> as the size of a grain of mustard seed, you could say to this mountain, move from here to another place and it will move; and <u>nothing will be impossible for you</u>." Matthew 17:19-20*

The above passage underscores a very important relationship between belief and faith. First, Jesus criticized his disciples for their "unbelief." Then, He stated that if they had believed, their action of speaking would have been enough to produce the results they wanted. *We believe first then we act in faith!*

• **Belief and Trust**

Apart from its religious applications, we sometimes use the word belief to express trust. Like belief, sometimes the word trust is used in everyday language in a feeble way. When we say that we trust, what we frequently mean is that we are uncertain. For example, when we say, "I trust that you will make it home alright," what we are really saying is that we are not certain that the person will arrive safely. However, in matters pertaining to God, whenever we use the word trust as it relates to belief we should mean a strong confidence in the reliability and faithfulness of God.

PRACTICES

In relation to faith, I choose to use the word practices meaning processing and carrying out ideas or plans. They are habits. I don't mean this in the sense of rehearsing. I don't believe that we practice our faith over and over in order to get better at a particular process. Rather, whenever we follow a specific course of action, the result will be similar no matter how many times it is repeated.

When we apply principles of belief to life situations, they become practices of faith. Practices of faith are about being practical and pragmatic as opposed to just being theoretical. *Merely believing in something doesn't make it happen necessarily all by itself.* It is a good idea to identify practices of faith with the meaningful adage, "God helps those who help themselves." Indeed, it is carrying out a plan for a desired result. If we know that God is faithful and dependable, then we must believe that when we duplicate procedures of faith the results will always be positive.

The phrase "through faith" is used in Hebrews chapter 11 four times. In verse 3, it refers to the *dynamic actions* of God. In verses 11, 28, and 33, it refers to the *dynamic actions* of people through God. These references complement the things I stated previously about faith.

Finally, the expression "by faith" is stated repeatedly in Hebrews Chapter 11 because each usage introduces various practices of faith. *These passages don't say by faith someone believed, but by faith someone did something!*

• **Practice and Prayer**

Frequently, the results of our prayers hinge on our practices of faith. In other words, prayer is often doing something about what we are requesting. For example, if someone prays for a job and gets one, the person would have to go to the place of employment in order to start working.

FAITH

Ordinarily, we use the word faith in many different ways. Like belief and trust, the most frequent use of the word faith is uttered without much conviction. Often when we make statements as, "I have faith that you will return," we are wishing that the person would return. In contrast to using the word faith in a weak way, the Bible uses the word faith, as I have already indicated, in association with strong and vibrant actions. When I use the word faith in this book, I'm referring to its biblical use.

In Matthew 8:5-13, a Roman military officer, who was a leader of a hundred men, came to Jesus strongly requesting help for one of his servants. The servant was paralyzed and seriously ill at home. Jesus responded that He would go to the house to heal the servant. The centurion said to Jesus that he knew it was not necessary for Him to go to the house to heal the employee. The centurion declared that just as he had authority over men, he believed that Jesus had authority over diseases. He said to Jesus, "But speak the word only, and my servant shall be healed." To this, Jesus responded, "I have not found so great faith, no, not even in Israel." Jesus added, "Go your way; and as you have believed, so it will done for you." The servant was healed immediately.

The centurion sincerely believed that Jesus could heal people when He was not in their presence. It was this belief that compelled the powerful officer who commanded many men to seek Jesus for help. However, the centurion's act of faith was that *he himself went to Jesus.*

In addition to what I previously stated about faith, the word faith in the Bible usually has specific indications. In the Old Testament, "faith" implies *faith in God.* In the New Testament, "faith" implies *faith in God through Jesus Christ.*

The people in the Old Testament did things in faith believing the promises of a Messiah to come. Hebrews 11:39 states, "And all these people, having obtained a good report through faith, did not receive the promise." Although they died before the Messiah came, they looked for eternal fellowship with God.

> *These people all died in faith not having received the promises but having*

seen them from far, were persuaded of them, embraced them, and admitted that they were strangers and pilgrims on earth. They who said such things declared plainly that they sought a country. Truly, if they had been mindful of that country where they came from they might have had opportunity to return. They desired a better country, that is, a heavenly place. What is important is that God was not ashamed to be called their God because He had prepared a city for them. Hebrews 11:13-16

Today, the underpinning of our faith is often connected to that of people in the Bible. God wanted to link their faith with ours. Referring to people of faith in the Old Testament, Hebrews 11: 40 states, "God provided a better thing for us that they without us should not be made perfect."

We look back at the people of faith in the Bible as examples for our faith. They expected us to continue in the legacies of their faith. Referring to people of faith in the Old Testament who are now our "witnesses," Hebrews 12:1 states,

> *Therefore, seeing that we are surrounded also by so great a cloud of witnesses, let us lay aside every weight, and the sin that so easily weigh us down, and let us run with patience the race that is placed before us.*

In the New Testament, we are encouraged to seek eternal fellowship with God through faith in Jesus.

> *Looking to Jesus the Author and Finisher of our faith, Who for the joy that was set before Him endured the cross, despised the shame, and sits at the right hand of the throne of God. Hebrews 12:2*

• **The Dynamics of Faith**

Since, biblically faith pertains to God who we cannot see; I do not think it is truly possible to define faith. We can't really define God therefore we can't really define faith. Moreover, since faith is accepted essentially as independent of our intellect and reasoning, if we could positively define faith, it would hardly be faith.

Although I don't think biblically we can basically define faith, we can express faith in the Bible in at least two ways. First, it is responding to God because of His assurance that He is concerned about us. Second, it is being positive that God responds to our actions that show confidence in Him. We can extract the previous two points from Hebrews 11:6, "He is a rewarder to them who diligently seek Him."

The ultimate biblical statement about faith is, "Now faith is the substance of things hoped for, the evidence of things not seen" (Hebrews 11:1). Still, this is not a definition of faith. *It does not tell us what faith is. It tells us what faith does!*

Introduction

What I have mentioned so far about faith are things relating to its dynamics. For more on this, here are some aspects of faith that are connected to its dynamics as expressed in Hebrews 11:1.

Faith is substantive. The word substance usually refers a tangible matter. Sometimes, it denotes something that has practical value. At other times, it means something of importance. These meanings relate well to the Greek word translated substance in Hebrews 11:1. The Greek meanings of the word in this text are "essence" and "confidence."

So, faith being a substance isn't abstract. It's the essence of what we believe. Indeed, it *materializes* the things we expect to receive from God. It is the stuff that makes our belief a reality!

Faith is hope. Hope, like belief, is used often in everyday talk to indicate doubtfulness. For instance, when we say "I hope it snows today," what we are really saying is that we are not sure that it will snow. We should never use hope in this way concerning God for two biblical reasons. First, words in the Bible translated "hope" essentially mean to expect or to trust. Second, when The King James Version of the Bible was written, the word "hope" fundamentally meant to have confidence or trust. It didn't mean necessarily the mere possibility of something happening.

Whatever we hope for through faith in God, we should believe that it is possible. Jesus, encouraging His followers to believe in what they hoped for, states in Matthew 19:26 that some things are impossible for people, "but with God all things are possible." In other words, when we trust God we can be *hopeful* about things that might look *hopeless* to others.

Since faith is something that is in action, in matters of faith, hope is not simply to desire something but to expect its fulfillment. In point of fact, hope in this context is an extraordinary conviction about God that *compels, impels and propels* a person to action.

Faith is the evidence of things not seen. The Greek word for evidence in Hebrews 11:1 definitely means conviction. It is proof or collaborating testimony of facts. Thus, evidence helps us to form conclusions. Also, it assists us to reach desirable resolutions.

Moreover, faith as evidence clearly *demonstrates* itself. Accordingly, the phrase in Hebrews 11:1, "the evidence of things not seen," *means that through faith we can actually see what we hope for before it happens!* Again, in Hebrews 11:3 we are told, "Through faith we understand that the worlds were framed by the word of God, so that things that are seen were not made of things that do appear." God created the universe we see from what was not visible. Believing this further encourages us to act through faith. What is more, as we begin to act through faith, we often start to see the results. *The "evidence of things" we did not see before we started to act!*

Consequently, in trying to understand faith, we should not try to know exactly what faith is like. Instead, we should strive to recognize the things we could do through faith. The mistake that many people make is that they try to understand life first so they might have faith, rather than have faith that they might understand life. This is to say that although we can't explain faith adequately or see the bases of our faith, nevertheless, we can see the results of faith.

In matters of faith, when believers in God don't know what a thing is, we shouldn't ask "what is this thing?" Rather, we should ask "what does this thing do?" This attitude makes us more practical and pragmatic. It makes us more productive in using what we have to achieve greater things in life. It gives us added confidence to accomplish more in life. Having said all this, how does faith work?

Well, our entire life should be based on faith. In other words, why bother to get up in the morning or even to cross the street? We do these things because we don't get a whole lot done if we stay in bed and we can't get to the other side of the street unless we cross over. Simply put, unless we do something we aren't likely to accomplish much.

What is more, faith doesn't depend on how we see our circumstances or conditions. What really matters is how we respond to stuff in our lives. This is another reason why I use the term "practices of faith" to mean doing by or through faith.

• Faith and Trust

We also use the word faith to express trust. Trust, as it relates to faith, sometimes means devotion and allegiance to a person or thing. In this book, when I use the word faith I'm also expressing loyalty, but only in the particular biblical sense of faithfulness to God through action. This kind of loyalty in the Bible reflects people's practices of faith.

• Faith and Typology

Typology is an important component of the Principles of Belief and Practices of Faith. Typology is the study or systematic classification of things that have characteristics or qualities in common. In scriptural studies, it is forecasting events using *types*. In the eleventh chapter of Hebrews, the experiences of all the people acting through faith involved typology. As a result, typology helps us to emulate biblical characters of faith.

Types Words translated from biblical languages meaning types include ensample or example, pattern, design, and figure. Usually, types are used in the Bible for interpreting previous scriptural events. That is, a type being a person or situation exemplifying a particular figure, representation, or symbol of something to come, such as an event in the Old Testament that foreshadows another in the New Testament.

There are several people in the Old Testament because of some of their characteristics and experiences, prefigure Jesus in the New Testament. For example, in Genesis 22:1-19, Isaac can be typed to Jesus because of quite a few facets of Abraham's attempt to sacrifice him to God. They include:

Isaac was called the "*only son*" of Abraham and the son who he *loved* (Genesis 22:2).

26

Introduction

Jesus was the *beloved* and *only begotten son* of God (Matthew 3:17 and John 3:16).

Isaac bore the wood to be burned on his back on which he was to be sacrificed (Genesis 22:6).
Jesus carried the cross on His back on which He was sacrificed (John 19:17).

Isaac was to be a *substitute for the sacrificial lamb* of the Old Testament (Genesis 22:2).
Jesus was called the *Sacrificial* "Lamb of God" (John 1:29).

Indeed, Jesus Himself interpreted that Old Testament using typology. For instance, in predicting elements of His death and resurrection, Jesus typed Jonah to Himself.

Then certain members of the scribes and of the Pharisees said, "Master, we would like to see a sign from You." Jesus answered, "An evil and adulterous generation seeks a sign. No sign

27

shall be given to it except the sign of the prophet Jonas. Because as Jonas was three days and three nights in the whale's belly, similarly, the Son of Man will be three days and three nights in the heart of the earth." Matthew 12:38-40

Furthermore, the Bible uses typologies to interpret itself. In Romans 5:14, a type is used to prophesy the coming of the Messiah.

Nevertheless, death reigned from Adam to Moses, even over them who had not sinned in similar ways to Adam's transgression, who is the figure of Him who was to come.

The Apostles Paul and Peter among other New Testament writers used types to interpret the Old Testament. Paul wrote in 1 Corinthians 10:1-7:

Moreover, brothers and sisters, I would not have you ignorant regarding the *fact that all our fathers were under the cloud and they all passed through the sea. They all were baptized through Moses in the cloud and in the sea. They all ate the same spiritual meat. They all drank the same spiritual drink, for they drank of that spiritual Rock that followed them, and that Rock was Christ. However, God was not pleased with many of them. Therefore, many of them died in the wilderness. Now these things were our <u>examples</u> to the intent that we should not lust after evil things as they also lusted. Do not become idolaters as were some of them. As it is written, "The people sat down to eat and drink, and rose up to play."*

In the above passage, the connection between Moses and Jesus is clear. The correlation between spiritual meat and drink to the Lord's Supper is also evident. Additionally, Paul was stating that things involved in the Hebrew people's experiences as they traveled through the wilderness were types relating to incidents that would occur in the life of Jesus. For example, when Paul mentioned "baptism in the cloud and sea," he was referring to two things: (1) the cloud that guided the Hebrew people as they traveled by day (Exodus 13:21), and (2) the parting of the waters of the Red Sea by God allowing the people to cross over on dry land (Exodus 14:21). These incidents were typed to Jesus' death and resurrection.

In the scripture below, Peter clearly used baptism as a metaphor to type Jesus' death and resurrection.

> The like figure where even baptism also now saves us (not the putting away of the filth of the flesh, but the answer of a good conscience toward God) by the resurrection of Jesus Christ.
> 1 Peter 3:21

Perhaps an easy way to grasp the basic significance of type is to know that it is derived from a Middle English word that means "symbol," and from a Latin word that means, "image." Although these denotations are important to the study of biblical typology, the meaning that is most essential is from biblical Greek. The Greek New Testament word *tupos* is related to the English word "type" as in "typecasting" and "typewriting." To typecast is to cast a person repeatedly in the same type of role, or to categorize things by the same kind, sort, or nature. The word typewrite was originally connected to the process of printing, making an impression (typing), or producing a *seal*. The connection between "seal" and "type" is quite significant to the practice of faith.

Seals Historically, seals were used to show a person's ownership of his or her possessions or to confirm that a thing was genuine. Often, seals were raised and engraved symbols or emblems on signet rings that were pressed into pieces of wax to make impressions. They were used also on official documents to certify signatures.

Today, seals are used sometimes to stamp documents indicating that an organization is authentic. They are still used to "seal" letters or packages to give confirmation or assurance that they are the genuine marks of an office. Seals, as well, are devices that close things tightly and securely preventing the entrance or exit of certain things such as liquid or air. Also, seals are devices placed on envelopes, parcels, containers and other such things. The seals must be broken to open them and can thus reveal tampering. In addition, "to seal," means to confirm a decision or come to an agreement on an issue.

The nuances of seal are important to believers for three reasons.

First, God's presence within us in the form of the Holy Spirit is a seal that guarantees our salvation and all that He has promised us. It is His mark of approval and seal of authenticity. Ephesians 1:14 states that the Holy Spirit is "the earnest of our inheritance until the redemption of the purchased possession, to the praise of His glory." "Earnest" of course, is a down payment, pledge or sign that confirms a contract for a future event.

Introduction

Second, according to the New Testament, the Holy Spirit seals believers.

> *In Whom you also trusted after you heard the word of truth, the gospel of your salvation. In Whom also after you believed, you were sealed with that Holy Spirit of Promise. Ephesians 1:13*

This means that God places the Holy Spirit within us as an indelible image of Himself. This secures God's commitment of salvation for us. "The Spirit itself bears witness with our spirit, that we are the children of God" (Romans 8:16).

Third, another way we could say, "filled" with the Holy Spirit is "sealed" with the Holy Spirit because the Holy Spirit is a striking impression of God's power that people see in us!

> *When they had prayed, the place was shaken where they were assembled. They were all filled with the Holy Spirit and they <u>spoke the word of God with boldness</u>. Acts 4:31*

A GUIDE TO SUCCESSFUL LIVING

On the basis of what I said previously about belief and faith, I extrapolated from the eleventh chapter of Hebrews a fundamental concept. My view is that events in this chapter underscore that belief is a thought while faith is acting on what is believed. I came to this conclusion by comparing the trials or triumphs of people of faith in Hebrews chapter 11 to various challenges or opportunities presently affecting Christians. In other words, *they are our types and we are sealed by their legacies of belief and faith.*

The purpose of this book, therefore, is to show that people of faith in the eleventh chapter of Hebrews, from Abel to Moses, represent *at least one Principle of Belief and one Practice of Faith.* These Principles of Belief and Practices of Faith *are our guide to successful living.*

PRINCIPLE AND PRACTICE ONE
Giving and Receiving

By faith Abel offered God a better sacrifice than Cain. The sacrifice witnessed to his righteousness. Actually, God said that Abel's gift was evidence of his righteousness. Although Abel is dead his faith still speaks to us. Hebrews 11:4

Hebrews 11:4 refers to an account in Genesis 4:2-7 about two brothers, Cain and Abel. "Abel was a keeper of sheep, but Cain was a tiller of the ground" (Genesis 4:2). Eventually, "Cain brought of the fruit of the ground an offering to the Lord" (Genesis 4:3). But, "Abel, he also brought of the firstlings of his flock and of the fat thereof" (Genesis 4:4). God accepted Abel's offering but rejected Cain's offering.

• **Firstlings**

The vital point of the story is that Abel brought the firstlings of his flock. Firstling means the first of a kind or category. It also means a first-born offspring. Genesis 4:4 indicates two things. First, Abel offered his first-born lambs, "firstlings," as his sacrifice to God. Second, Abel included the best parts of the lambs, "of the fat thereof," in the sacrifice. Therefore, the verse infers that he sacrificed his best lambs. This was an act of faith because generally the best animals were kept for breeding. He depended on God to supply his needs from the sheep that remained in the flock.

The Scripture does not mention anything in particular about Cain's sacrifice. Hence, the story infers that Cain did not give God the first or best produce of his harvest. Apparently, he brought what he wanted to spare. At most, he brought God his leftovers.

Obviously, the story of Cain and Abel shows that we should give God our best. The Bible provides several elements that complement the model of giving "firstlings."

• Tithes

The concept and practice of tithing are fundamentals of the story concerning Abel's sacrifice to God. In the Old Testament tithes were offerings or sacrifices to God of one tenth of one's produce. Here are five things that constitute tithes in the Old Testament.

1. Tithes involved firstlings.

   There you shall bring your burnt offerings, sacrifices, tithes, heave offerings of your hand, vows, freewill offerings, and the firstlings of your herds and flocks. Deuteronomy 12:6

2. Tithes were mandated in the Old Testament.

Principles of Belief and Practices of Faith

As soon as the commandment came abroad, the children of Israel brought in abundantly the firstfruits of corn, wine, oil, honey, all the increase of the field, and the tithe of all things.
2 Chronicles 31:5

3. Tithes were given at prescribed times to the priesthood, marginalized people, and the poor in the community.

   When you have made an end of tithing all the tithes of your increase of the third year, which is the year of tithing, give it to the Levite, the stranger, the fatherless, and the widow, that they may eat within your gates and be filled. Deuteronomy 26:12

4. Tithes provided for the temple.

   Everyone should bring all the tithes into the storehouse, that there may be food in My house, and prove Me by this, says the Lord of hosts, if I will not open the windows of heaven for you, and pour out for you a blessing, that there shall not be room enough to receive it. Malachi 3:10

5. Tithing was comprehensive, exhaustive, and inclusive.

All the tithes of the land, whether of the seed of the land, or of the fruit of the tree, is the Lord's. It is holy to the Lord. Leviticus 27:30

• **Abraham and Tithing**

The biblical patriarch Abraham whose story is told in Genesis chapters 11-25 is our "spiritual father of faith." For this reason, his example of tithing is important to us.

Therefore it is of faith, that it might be by grace, to the end the promise

*might be sure to all the descendants;
not only to those who are of the law,
but to those also who are of the faith
of Abraham, who is the father of us all.
Romans 4:16*

In the fourteenth chapter of Genesis, Abram (Abraham) gave tithes to King Melchizedek after being blessed by him.

*Melchizedek king of Salem brought
out bread and wine. He was the
priest of the highest God. He blessed
Abram, saying, "Blessed be Abram of
the highest God, Possessor of heaven
and earth; and blessed be the highest God, Who has delivered your enemies into your hand." Then Abram
gave Melchizedek tithes of everything.
Genesis 14:18-20*

• **Melchizedek as a Type of Christ**

Melchisedec, king of Salem, priest of the highest God, met Abraham returning from the slaughter of the kings, and blessed him. Abraham gave a tenth part of everything he had to Melchizedec. Melchizedec, first being by interpretation king of righteousness, and after that also king of Salem, that is, king of peace. He was without father, without mother, without descent, having neither beginning of days, nor end of life, but made like the Son of God; is a priest continually. Now consider how great this man was, to whom even the patriarch Abraham gave the tenth of the spoils. Hebrews 7:1-4

Melchizedek name literally means righteous king. He was from Salem, a place whose name means peace. He was a mysterious person without record of his birth and without parents or ancestry. He was an everlasting priest. There-fore, he was like the son of God. These things made him a type of Jesus Christ (see Hebrews 7:11).

It was significant that Abraham paid tithes to a priest. According to Numbers 18:21, the people paid tithes to the Levitical priests for services.

> *See, I have given the children of Levi all the tenth in Israel for an inheritance for their service, even the service of the tabernacle of the congregation.*

The Levites were descendants of Abraham through Isaac and Jacob (Genesis 29:34). They were associated with Moses' brother, Aaron, the high priest (Numbers 3:9-10, 18:7-11). These Old Testament passages indicate three facts about tithes and the priesthood.

1. Although he was an ancestor of the Lev-ites, Jacob himself was not a priest. Yet, Jacob being thankful to God for His

promise of blessings to him and his descendants, pledged to tithe to God. Jacob said, "And this stone, which I have set for a pillar, shall be God's house; and of all that you shall give me I will surely give the tenth to you" (Genesis 28:22). The implication is that the practice of tithing was generational for both the givers and receivers. Of course, the office of the priesthood was inherited from generation to generation.

2. Jacob lived before Aaron the first official priest. The priesthood of Melchizedek came before Aaron. Therefore, Melchizedek was superior to Aaron. The inference is that tithing supersedes the office of the priesthood.

3. Tithing existed before Moses and the Old Testament Laws. Abraham tithed to Melchizedek out of gratitude and not out of the requirements of the Mosaic Laws. Melchizedek's authority to receive tithes represented something greater than the Mosaic Laws.

Additionally, from the New Testament we gather several important points about the priesthood and tithing through typologies in Hebrews 7:1-28.

- Melchizedek did not descend from the lines of Aaronic and Levitical priests (see Psalms 115:10, 12, 118:3, 135:19; Hebrews 7:11-17; I Chronicles 12:27, 27:17). The priesthood was not instituted until hundreds of years of later (see Hebrews 7:4-14).

- Melchizedek priesthood preceded the Mosaic Laws (see Hebrews 7:9-16). Melchizedek, being a priest, had the power to bless (see Hebrews 7:6-17).

- In keeping with the Old Testament Law the Levites collected tithes from the people (see Numbers 18:21). The Levites and the Israelites were all descendants of Abraham (see Hebrews 7:4-10).

Giving and Receiving

- Figuratively, since Melchizedek received tithes from Abraham, then Levi, his descendant, paid tithes also to Melchizedek (see Hebrews 7:4-10).

- Melchizedek blessed Abraham; therefore, he blessed Levi as well. This means that the blessing of tithing reaches down through generations (see Hebrews 7:4-10).

- The one who blesses because of receiving tithes is always greater than the person who is blessed as a consequence of giving tithes. Therefore, Melchizedek was greater than Levi (see Hebrews 7:5-10).

- The Levitical priests were men who eventually died. Jesus is alive. Jesus was not a direct descendant of Levi. Jesus descended from the family line of Abraham. Still, Jesus fulfilled the prophecy of Psalm 110:4, "The Lord has sworn, and will not repent; You are a priest for ever after the order of Melchizedek." Since Melchizedek was superior to Levi, Jesus was therefore superior to Levi, and the Levitical Laws of the priesthood (see Hebrews 7:8-28).

■ Ultimately, tithing is a high calling of God to the point that we can confidently say that when we tithe we are tithing to God through Jesus Christ who lives (see Hebrews 7:1-10).

• The Passover

The narrative of Cain and Abel in Genesis 4:2-7, involves another important factor of tithing. Abel was a herdsman, so he brought cattle as sacrifice to God. Cain was a farmer, for that reason he brought the produce of the field. It has been suggested that Abel brought a sacrifice that involved the shedding of blood and that made the difference to God. That doesn't seem right since it wouldn't be fair to expect a farmer to bring an animal sacrifice.

However, as a result of Abel's act of faith, the shedding of the blood of sacrificial animals often became significant typologies. An example of this is the Passover. The Passover commemorates the deliverance of God's people out of bondage in Egypt.

In the tenth day of this month every head of a household shall take a lamb, according to the house of their ancestors; a lamb for each household. If the household is too little for the lamb, let the people of the household and their next door neighbor take the lamb according to the number of the people; every person according to his or her eating shall make your count for the lamb. Your lamb shall be without blemish, a male of the first year; you shall take it out from the sheep, or from the goats. You shall keep it up until the fourteenth day of the same month then the entire assembly of the congregation of Israel shall kill it in the evening. They shall take the blood, and smear it on the two side posts and on the upper door posts of the houses, wherein they shall eat it. Thus shall you eat it; with your loins girded, your shoes on your feet, and your staff in your hand. You shall eat it in haste. It is the Lord's Passover. I will pass through the land of Egypt tonight and will kill all the firstborn in the land of Egypt, both human and beast. Against all the gods of Egypt I will execute judgment. I am the Lord. The blood shall be to you for a token on the houses where you are; that when I see the blood, I will pass over you, and the plague shall not be on you to destroy you when I smite the land of Egypt. Today shall be to you a memorial. You shall keep it a feast to the Lord through all your generations. You shall keep it as a feast by My ordinance forever. Exodus 12: 3-8, 11-14

Giving and Receiving

Jesus is typed to the Passover lamb several times in the Bible. Here are two instances. First, at Jesus' baptism John the Baptist referred to Him as "The Lamb of God Who takes away the sin of the world" (John 1:29). Then, after Jesus' death and resurrection, I Peter 1:19 states, "The precious blood of Christ, as of a lamb without blemish and without spot," caused us to be born again.

Hence, Jesus fulfilled the requirements of the Old Testament Passover lamb. For example, we can easily conclude that since Jesus was sinless He was therefore without "blemish." Also, He was a male and was crucified about the time of the Passover.

Moreover, Jesus fulfilled at least one prophecy of the Passover lamb. According to Exodus 12:46 and Numbers 9:12, no "bone" of the Passover lamb was to be broken. The legs of Jesus were not broken on the cross.

When Jesus therefore had received the vinegar, He said, "It is finished." Then He bowed His head and died. The Jews therefore, because it was the Passover, did not want the bodies to remain on the cross on the Sabbath day (for that Sabbath was a high holy day). They besought Pilate that their legs might be broken, and that they might be taken away. Then came the soldiers, and broke the legs of the one of the men, and of the other man who was crucified with Jesus. But when they came to Jesus and saw that He was dead already, they did not break His legs. Instead, one of the soldiers with a spear pierced His side and instantly blood and water flowed out. He that saw it was a witness. His record is true. He knows that what he said is true, so that you might believe. For these things were done that the Scripture should be fulfilled, "A bone of Him shall not be broken." John 19:30-36

Finally, when Christians partake in the Communion of Christ, among other things, they fulfill the purpose of The Old Testament com- memoration of the Passover by celebrating Jesus' sacrificial death and resurrection. I Corinthians 5:7 states, "For even Christ our Passover is sacrificed for us."

• **Former and Latter Rains**

Rain, of course, is critical to an agricultural society. The timing of the rain is also important. There are two rainy seasons in Palestine. The Bible refers to the fall rains as the "former rain" (early rains) and the spring rains as the "latter rain" (later rains).

The Bible states that God gave the people the rains at the proper times. Here are two references:

> *"Let us now fear the Lord our God, Who gives rain, both the former and the latter, in His season. He reserves for us the appointed weeks of the harvest. Jeremiah 5:24*

I will give you the rain of your land in his due season, the first rain and the latter rain, that you may gather in your corn, your wine, and your oil. Deuteronomy 11:14

The former rain helped to prepare the ground for plowing and sowing and the latter rain helped the maturing of crops. Consequently, the people depended on adequate rain in the fall for a good harvest in the spring. The former and latter rains are therefore typologies of tithing.

Often, people tithe only when they are going through difficulties and want to be blessed. However, the former rain as a metaphor shows that God gives us His best at the proper times. This should motivate us to tithe consistently since we are constantly being blessed by God at the proper times.

Frequently, people feel that they are giving a lot when they tithe. All the same, the latter rain as a metaphor shows that God increases our blessings when we tithe. Like sowing and

Giving and Receiving

reaping, we depend on God for the "increase." First, God blesses us with seeds to plant crops. Then, He gives us the rains for them to grow!

What is more, through the metaphors of rains, we know that God promises the out-pouring of bountiful blessings on us.

> *Be glad then, you children of Zion, and rejoice in the Lord your God, for He has given you the former rain moderately, and He will cause to come down for you the rain, the former rain, and the latter rain in the first month. And the floors shall be full of wheat, and the vats shall overflow with wine and oil. Joel 2:23-24*

It is worth noting that closely following the above passage is a promise that can be typed to the outpouring of the Holy Spirit.

> *It shall come to pass that I will pour out My Spirit upon all flesh; and your sons and your daughters shall prophesy,*

your old men shall dream dreams, and your young men shall see visions. Joel 2:28

• **Firstfruits**

Proverbs 3:9 states, "Honor the Lord with your substance, and with the firstfruits of all your increase." Firstfruits were portions of the first ripened fruits or grains of harvest that the Israelites gave God. Firstfruits also meant the choicest produce of the land first harvested (the first of the firstfruits), or even processed products such as wool.

Actually, the Bible states that the first of all things belongs to God. These things include people and animals (Exodus 13:2-16; Numbers 3:12-16). Additionally, firstfruits were thanksgiving offerings for the support the priests (Deuteronomy 18:1-4). These types of thanksgiving offerings were acts of tithing (Nehemiah 10:36-37).

When someone gave firstfruits to God that person acknowledged, "The earth is the Lord's and all that is in it; the world, and they who dwell therein" (Psalm 24:1). The person gave back to God what was God's in the first place so that God would bless them with more. First-fruits offering could be done on behalf of individuals (Exodus 23:19; Deuteronomy 26:1-11), or the nation (Leviticus 23:10, 17).

Firstfruits as Meal Offerings. Beyond the tithing of produce, the first or best results of blessings belonged to God. Such as, after a person tithed from a produce, what was used of the remainder of the produce as an offering to God had to come from the best of the finished product. For instance, if someone baked bread as an offering to God, the first loaf of the first batch made from new grain was presented to God. In this sense, the act of offering firstfruits was implied. "You shall offer up a cake of the first of your dough for a special donation; as you do the special donation of the threshing floor, so shall you give it" (Numbers 15:20).

Israel as Firstfruits. Israel was referred to as the firstfruits of God's harvest.

*Israel was holy to the Lord and the first-
fruits of His increase… Jeremiah 2:3*

This is a typology for Christians for two reasons.

1. The church is blessed because *it
    is Israel as prophesied in the Old
    Testament (Psalm 115:12)*.
2. In the New Testament *the church
    is called Israel(Galatians 6:16)*.

A direct New Testament connection of
firstfruits to tithing is found in Hebrews 7:4.
Referring to Melchizedek, the king-priest,
it states, "Now consider how great this man
was, to whom even the patriarch Abraham
gave the tenth of the spoils." The word translated "spoils" in this verse literally means
"firstfruits."

Jesus as Firstfruits. The first celebration
of firstfruits was at the Passover (Leviticus
23:10-14; Exodus 23:16). I mentioned previ-

ously that I Corinthians 5:7 states that Jesus is our Passover. Connecting Jesus to firstfruits, I Corinthians 15:23 states, "Every person in his own order: Christ the firstfruits; afterward they who are Christ's at His coming." Consequently, firstfruits offerings are typed to Jesus through the Passover.

The Holy Spirit as Firstfruits. Seven weeks after the celebration of the Passover came the second firstfruits celebration known as Pentecost (Exodus 34:22; Numbers 28:26). Of course, in Acts 2 it was at Pentecost that the disciples received the blessing of the baptism of the Holy Spirit. Therefore, the Holy Spirit can be typed to firstfruits. "And not only they, but ourselves also, who have the firstfruits of the Spirit, even we ourselves groan within ourselves, waiting for the adoption, that is, the redemption of our body" (Romans 8:23).

Christians as Firstfruits. Remarkably, the New Testament describes Christians as firstfruits in at least four ways.

Principles of Belief and Practices of Faith

First, we are firstfruits through Jesus Christ.

Of His own will He created us with the word of truth, that we should be a kind of firstfruits of His creatures. James 1:18

Second, the first converts to Christianity in a church are firstfruits.

Likewise greet the church that is in their house. Salute my well beloved Epaenetus, who is the firstfruits of Achaia unto Christ. Romans 16:5

Third, the first converts of an area are firstfruits.

I implore you, brethren, (you know the house of Stephanas, that it is the firstfruits of Achaia, and that they have addicted themselves to the ministry of the saints). I Corinthians 16:15

Giving and Receiving

Fourth, Christians in the Bible who did not return to immorality after being converted were called firstfruits.

> *These are those who were not defiled with women; they are virgins. These are those who follow the Lamb wherever He goes. These were redeemed from among the people, they are firstfruits to God and to the Lamb. Revelation 14:4*

Finally, the New Testament portrays the Old Testament people who were righteous before God as firstfruits. Those who lived for God before Christianity were given to God as firstfruits of which Christians are now part of the whole offering.

> *If casting them away is the reconciling of the world, what shall the receiving of them be, but life from the dead? Because the firstfruit is holy, the lump is*

also holy; and if the root is holy, so are the branches. Romans 11: 15-16

• **The Priesthood of Believers**

Many Christians do not believe that we need priests to intercede for us before God. Jesus is our high priest and intercessor. "Jesus our forerunner has entered and has been made a high priest for ever after the order of Melchisedec" (Hebrews 6:20). There are numerous other biblical references to Jesus as high priest that we can look at. Here are two. They are Hebrews 3:1 and 4:14. See also the text of Hebrews 5:1-10.

In fact, many Christians believe that we are now the priesthood of God. "You also, as lively stones, are part of a spiritual house, a holy priesthood, to offer up spiritual sacrifices, acceptable to God by Jesus Christ" (I Peter 2:5). Consequently, our acts of tithing produce a spiritual environment that touches and encourages others to give.

Giving and Receiving

Some people often resist paying tithes because they see church leaders receiving the benefits of such offerings. However, this is acceptable to God. Those who serve the people in our churches are in the legacy of the descendants of Levi.

> *Certainly, they that are of the sons of Levi, who receive the office of the priesthood, have a commandment to take tithes of the people according to the law, that is, of their brothers and sisters, although they are the offspring of Abraham. Hebrews 7:5*

Furthermore, since we are now the priests of God, we all benefit from tithing. Through the legacy of Abraham tithing to Melchizedek, the blessings are passed from generation to generation. This insinuates that our tithes will bless even our children not yet conceived!

> *Melchisedec was not descended from Levi but he received tithes from*

Abraham, and blessed him who had the promises. Without a doubt, the lesser is blessed by the greater. Priests received tithes from people who later died. But, Melchisedec received tithes from one who lives. And if I may say so, Levi also paid tithes to Melchisedec because he was the genetic material of his father, Abraham, when Melchisedec met him. Hebrews 7:6-10

Usually, a tithing church provides for future generations because it is free of the shackles of debts. Commonly, churches where members do not tithe pass on debts from generation to generation.

• Giving in the New Testament Church

Giving in the New Testament Church drew from the Old Testament practice of tithing with regard to giving a portion to the poor.

Giving and Receiving

The Apostle Paul gave clarity to this when he wrote, "Now concerning the collection for the saints, as I have given orders to the churches of Galatia, you do the same" (1 Corinthians 16:1). The "saints" in this verse were mostly church members who were poor. This was particularly true of churches in Jerusalem.

Actually, part of the Paul's commission by the Council at Jerusalem was to help the poor.

> But on the contrary, when they saw that the gospel of those who were Gentiles was committed to me, as the gospel of those who were not Gentiles was to Peter; (for He who effectively promoted Peter to the apostleship of those who were not Gentiles, the Same was mighty in me toward the Gentiles). James, Cephas, and John, who seemed to be pillars, perceived the grace that was given to me, so they gave me and Barnabas the right hands of fellowship; that we should go to the Gentiles, and they to those who were

not Gentiles. Only they asked that we remember the poor in Jerusalem... Galatians 2:7-10

• **Tithing and Giving Today**

Many Christians struggle with whether or not they should tithe. Yet, there is no question that most churches would be more effective in ministry and service if only a significant amount of their members would tithe. Indeed, it is a poor testimony to the world when God's places of worship and ministries don't have sufficient funds for their functions and upkeep.

What we gather from the Old Testament is that we should tithe from our gross income rather than from net pay. It also means that is it important not to give God our scraps or odds and ends. Often, we give things such as furniture and appliances that we don't want to the church.

Churches suffer because of what I call the "spirit of insufficient giving." Their members give only for the bare necessities and at the last resort. As a result, there is not much planning for the future. Too often, meager fundraisings become the norm providing an excuse to give little. Consequently, churches remain in a "Babylonian Captivity" whereby the churches are in ruins and its best talents and resources are deported into the "world." By saying this, I'm making an analogy to the destruction of Jerusalem by the Babylonians and the deportation of selected people to Babylon as described in 2 Kings 24 and 2 Chronicles 36.

When members tithe consistently, the yoke of the "Babylonian Captivity" is broken. More people become active in ministries and more people donate their talents and time.

Finally, a tithing church can expect miracles. The problems of the church will change from lack to stack. The church will literally run out of room to stack God's blessings (see Malachi 3:10), because it will be blessed repeatedly.

Give, and it shall be given to you; good measure, pressed down, shaken together, and running over, shall people give into your bosom. For with the same measure that you compute, it shall be measured to you again. Luke 6:38

• **Proportional Giving**

In the New Testament Church, the practices of giving went beyond tithing. The Early Church interpreted tithing in the Old Testament as a precursor to a better way of giving. Members were encouraged to *give in proportion* to their blessings. We have a picture of this when Paul wrote,

On the first day of the week everyone must give <u>as God has prospered you</u> so that there will be no collections when I come. I Corinthians 16:2

Some churches in which much tithes are given, eventually grow to have a significant amount of their membership give in proportion of their blessings. Those members do not limit their giving to God since He does not limit

His giving to us. They give beyond 10 percent of their earnings because they are blessed to live successfully on less than 90 percent of their income. Indeed, the more we are blessed the more we should give.

• **Sharing**

Tithing and giving proportionally in the church are also about pooling our resources to share with each other as well as others who are not members or even Christians. In essence, this is in keeping with the spirit of giving in the New Testament Church.

> *All who believed were together, and had all things in common; and sold their possessions and goods, and parted them to all people, as every person had need. They, continuing daily with one accord in the temple, and breaking bread from house to house, did eat their food with gladness and singleness of heart. Acts 2:44-46*

In the end, sharing is really investing with no risk since we benefit from the additional blessings God gives to the church. Incidentally, among other things, sharing is the basis of good citizenship, government, and business.

• Giving is Receiving

Tithing and proportional giving encourage us to be kind since we benefit from our giving. In Acts 20:35, Paul stated that Jesus said, "It is more blessed to give than to receive." We don't necessarily give to people in order to receive from others but we certainly don't lack because we give. Regardless, we cannot give what we do not have. And, if giving makes us get more to give, then we are blessed!

• Giving and Receiving is Forgiving

We are more likely as well to forgive because of giving and receiving God's blessings. The

Sabbatical Laws or Forgiveness Laws found in Leviticus 25:1-15 indicate that no one should indefinitely own anything. *And, no one should indefinitely owe anything!* Obviously, these things again suggest that everything belongs to God.

According to the Sabbatical Laws, planting and reaping were to done for six years then in the seventh (Sabbatical) year the land would be given rest. God provided enough food in the planting years to last the entire sabbatical year. After seven sabbatical years, there was to be a jubilee year. In this year of celebration, all properties were returned to their original owners or descendants. Incidentally, the jubilee year started on the Day of Atonement, the day when God forgave the sins of the people.

• A Witness for God

The meaning of the word "witness" is another important component for understanding the Principle of Belief and Practice of Faith of Giving and Receiving. I mean *witness* in the sense of *a source of continuous evidence.* Hebrews 11:4 tells us that Abel still speaks to us because his "witness" endures beyond his death. Hebrews 7: 6-10 tells us that Melchizedek was a "witness" to God's power through tithing. Melchizedek's act of receiving tithes from Abraham was symbolic of that which is everlasting. Every tithe that is ever paid is offered in the same spirit of Abel's giving. Every tithe that is ever accepted is received in the same spirit in which Melchizedek acknowledged Abraham's offering. I suppose that when we are alive forever with Christ, our continuous praise to God will replace our tithes.

We should realize then that the word to "witness" doesn't always mean to "testify." It's not always the things we say about God to others that are most effective, rather, to be an effective witness for God is to make people see in us the enduring power of God to bless through the regular and ordinary things we do every day. Specifically, our witness through the Principle of Belief and Practice of Faith of Giving and Receiving is that by our giving, people will see that we are constantly receiving blessings from God.

• **Reciprocity**

There is a factor to giving and receiving that is supported by the Bible that I term *reciprocity*. Simply put, our spirit of giving largely determines what we receive back.

In Luke 6:38, Jesus spoke about this in a material sense.

> *Give and it shall be given to you…because with the same measure that you compute, it shall be measured to you again.*

In Galatians 6:7-8, Paul spoke about it in a spiritual sense.

> *Be not deceived, God is not mocked; because whatever a person sows, that shall he or she also reap. For the*

person who sows to his flesh shall of the flesh reap corruption; but he or she who sows to the Spirit shall of the Spirit reap life everlasting.

Based on the "witness" concept of giving and receiving, I suggest that "reciprocity" is tied to generational blessings. So, when our spirits of giving and receiving don't conform to the will of God we could affect the blessings of our descendants.

You shall not bow down to them, nor serve them. I am the Lord your God. I am a jealous God, recalling the iniquity of your ancestors to the third and fourth generations of them who hate Me... Deuteronomy 5:9

On the other hand, if our spirits of giving and receiving conform to the will of God our descendants will be blessed.

Giving and Receiving

You shall not bow down to them, nor serve them. I am the Lord your God. I am a jealous God, recalling the iniquity of your ancestors to the third and fourth generations of them who hate Me; <u>showing mercy to thousands of them who love Me and keep My commandments</u>. Deuteronomy 5:9-10

PRINCIPLE AND PRACTICE TWO
Role Modeling

By faith Enoch was translated that he should not see death; and was not found, because God had translated him, for before his translation he had this testimony, that he pleased God. Hebrews 11:5

Genesis 5:22 says, "Enoch walked with God." The exact phrase is repeated in Genesis 5:24. The repetition emphasizes that the fellowship Enoch had with God was exemplary and complementary. In the contexts of Genesis 5: 22 and 24, the basic Hebrew meaning of the word "walk" is "to live."

- ## **Walking with God**

Hebrews 11:5 states,

By faith Enoch was translated that he should not see death; and was not found, because God had translated him, for before his translation he had this testimony, that he pleased God.

Although the word "walk" is not used in Hebrews 11:5, the word "testimony" conveys a basic understanding of a Greek word for "walk." It means that which surrounds us. Therefore, walking with God means to live "surrounded by God."

Enoch walked with God by his life of *testimony* to the faithfulness of God. The name Enoch itself means that he dedicated his life to God. Enoch's way of living was completely devoted to the service and worship of God. His life gave proof that God exists. Enoch was a role model for God!

• **Testimony**

The principle and practice of role modeling is more than testifying that we believe in God because He has been good to us. We should testify about God just based on the fact that He exists. Moreover, if we can testify about the good things that happen to us, then we should also testify to the goodness of God when terrible things happen to us. Role modeling for God is not just what we say about Him but how we live in faithful witness for Him. This is Enoch's legacy for us.

To testify is to attest to something that can be proven. Enoch's long life of faithfulness to God was proven when God took him in a special way at death.

> *By faith Enoch was translated that he should not see death; and was not found, because God had translated him, for before his translation he had this testimony, that he pleased God. Hebrews 11:5*

Enoch's translation is a typology that points out another proof that we have an "earnest" or assurance of everlasting life. Accordingly, living like Enoch is like tasting heaven before we get there. We see this in Ephesians 1:13-14.

> *In Whom you also trusted, after that you heard the word of truth, the gospel of your salvation, in Whom also after you believed, you were <u>sealed</u> with that holy Spirit of Promise, Who is the <u>earnest</u> of our inheritance until the redemption of the purchased possession, to the praise of His glory.*

• **Pleasing God**

> *For before his translation he had this testimony, that he pleased God. Hebrews 11:5*

Through the above verse we understand that Enoch pleased God by fellowshipping with Him. Many people probably don't think that we can please God. Yet, God desires that we have a close relationship with Him. That is why He created us.

> *But without faith it is impossible to please Him…*
> *Hebrews 11:6*

The above verse tells us that in order to please God we must have faith. Since Enoch pleased God, his walk with God in fellowship was therefore faith.

• **The Existence of God**

> *Everyone who comes to God must believe that He is. Hebrews 11:6*

To have a model relationship with God like Enoch's we must believe unconditionally that God exists. This is more than just supposing that God is, or even proposing possibilities of His existence.

Historically, some philosophers, theologians, and lay people have argued for the existence of God. Here are five of perhaps the most common arguments that affect people, including Christians, even to this day.

a. *The Teleological Argument* This argument proposes that there is design in the universe that indicates order and purpose. This proves that there is a God. This reasoning, however, makes God mechanical, and even predictable. Actually, space is pretty disruptive. For instance, there is tremendous violence such as geomagnetic storms, astronomical eruptions, and solar flares in the universe. Indeed, it is believed that new worlds and their beauty are created through explosions! Thus, belief and faith in God must go beyond symmetries and consistencies in the universe.

b. *The Ontological Argument* This position basically states that we can't conceive a greater or a more perfect being than God. One of the problems in trying to prove that God exists this way is that this argument depends on our conception of who God is. Regardless of how God might affect our concept of Him, this process of thinking undermines the principle of belief and the practice of faith epitomized by Enoch. It certainly doesn't include in its reasoning the type of "experience" that Enoch had with God. God is independent of our thinking, even thinking of Him. Therefore, experiencing God is more significant than merely thinking about Him.

c. *The Moral Argument* This argument says that there is morality in the world because there is a God. Nevertheless, morality for many people is situational and relative. For many Christians during the Civil Rights Movement of the 1960's, segregation laws were certainly immoral. For other Christians, many segregation practices were moral because they were state laws in a country under God. Since what might be morally right for some people may not be for others, and what might be morally correct in a given situation for some people may not be for others, God is poorly described through morals alone. Maybe, a better way to show people that God is alive is to make our belief in God guide our faith. In other words, if we believe in God, and at the same time, we are inconsistent with our morals, we might just lead some people to think that God Himself is immoral.

d. *The Cosmological Argument* This frequently used argument for the existence of God states that we should believe in the existence of God because we can see His great works. Something or someone had to create what we see, particularly, the wonder and beauty of the universe. However, we must believe that God exists whether or not we see the celestial bodies. Furthermore, God is independent of our knowledge of Him. In other words, God existence does not depend on what we know of Him through his creations. After all, He has created everything including our knowledge. What is more, our knowledge of all that exists is limited. The very fact that we are always learning new things tends to prove this. As a result, the cosmological case for proving God is also limited. That is to say, how can we offer proof of a limitless God with limited minds? Ultimately, unless we have a belief and trust relationship with God like Enoch's, there is always the danger that viewing God only through the cosmos may make us relate more to creation than the Creator.

e. *The Biblical Argument* Possibly, most Christians simply point to the Bible as proof of God's existence. But there is no argument in the Bible for the existence of God! This was not needed since based on the biblical perspectives of belief and faith it was a given fact that God existed. It makes sense therefore that there are biblical statements that promote the existence of God as a *given truth*. Psalms 10:4 states, "the wicked" (the unbeliever) does not care or think about God. In other words, God exists whether or not people deny His existence. Also, Psalm 14:1 says that it is foolish to say that there is no God. This is another way of saying that proving the existence of God is not sensible. Moreover, when Psalm 19 states, "the heavens declare the glory of God; and the universe shows His handiwork," it is not proclaiming an argument for the existence of God, rather it "declares" who God is. Actually, biblical statements regarding the reality of God are mainly against polytheism not atheism. God demanded that people worship Him and not other gods (Exodus 20:3). The issue was not *whether or not God existed.* Finally, we could say that all these arguments trying to prove that God exists may not be in themselves proving that a single God exists as much as unintentionally giving the impression that there are many gods. Through belief and faith, God is, period!

• **Theodicy**

Theodicy is any argument defending God's goodness despite the existence of such things as pain, suffering, and evil. It seeks to answer the question: How can a good God allow bad things to happen to good people?

Believing in the goodness of God demands that we do so in spite of calamitous, catastrophic, or even cataclysmic events. If we believe that God is responsible for the magnificence of the earth, we must believe in a good God notwithstanding such horrors as famine, wars, earthquakes, hurricanes, and tornadoes. If we accept God for the beauty and wonders of the universe, then we must believe in His benevolence in spite of the ferocity of space storms, the collisions of galactic bodies, and the unthinkable consequences of being trapped in a black hole.

Similarly, as role models for God our world is not perfect. Even with a close relationship with God we are still subject to trials and tribulations. Additionally, our families and friends may endure disappointments, failures, disasters and tragedies. Still, the essence of Enoch's type of role modeling for God is to show that God is good under all circumstances. Whether we can explain or justify theodicy is irrelevant to us as role models for God. God does not ask us to defend Him. Really, how can we argue better for God other than being a role model for Him. Obviously, the storms will come but "through it all" we will just continue to live for God.

I think for believers what is relevant to the goodness of God is the answer to the question: To what extent do we believe in God? For instance, we might believe that God can heal some diseases like high blood pressure which generally can be effectively controlled or even cured. On the other hand, we might believe that God can do little against the present incurable pandemic of AIDS. Since God is supernatural, then nothing is "too hard" for God (Jeremiah 32:27), and everything is "possible" for God (Matthew 19:26).

• **Faith Crises**

We sometimes blame our problems and those of the world on God. For believers this often happens when we are going through faith crises. Faith crises can be defined as conditions in which our belief in God is shattered because of traumatic experiences. They paralyze our faith. Sometimes, we can over-come faith crises by developing a strong "Enoch type" relationship with God or drawing from the inner strength of such a relationship.

• **Blaming the Devil**

We often blame too many of the problems in the world on the devil. For instance, blaming the devil for widespread hunger in the world may be a poor excuse for our failure to do more for starving people as a whole. We also blame the devil for too many of our problems. For example, some people have poor health result-ing from eating unhealthy foods. This is not necessarily the work of the devil. Poor health for numerous people comes from choosing and eating too many of the wrong foods.

The devil is not mentioned in regard to Enoch's walk with God. Enoch's relationship with God is too encompassing and solid to in-clude the devil. When we develop such a re-lationship with God, the devil will have little importance in our lives. In other words, who we make important is God not satan.

• **Prayers**

And that He is a Rewarder of them who diligently seek Him. Hebrews 11:6

There are at least five attitudes that we bring to prayer at times that suggest we truly do not believe that God rewards us for diligently seeking Him.

First, we often pray repeatedly for the same things. There is at least one reason for this. That is, we usually want God to answer our prayer in a specific manner. We fail to recognize God's answer if it is different from our expectation. Actually, we do not want to accept the answer or do not truly believe that the answer is correct. If we can only believe God for the answer that we are seeking, then we don't believe unconditionally that He rewards those who diligently seek Him. Perhaps, there are times when we pray to God that we may not realize

89

that seeking Him with diligence means seeking Him sincerely. We are honest with God when we pray without any form of doubt and when we accept the answers He gives us.

Second, we often pray as if we are gambling. Frequently, these are prayers of desperation. God becomes our "last resort." This implies that we might be thinking, maybe "maybe there is a God," let me give prayer a "shot." Indeed, we pray like we "have nothing to lose." We should not approach God in prayer with the idea that if "we haven't got a prayer we haven't got a chance." It is not by chance that God answers prayers; rather He "rewards" all truthful prayers that are in His will. In other words, God blesses us with what is best for us.

Third, we seem to pray to God only when things are bad for us. What is really bad is this type of attitude to God. If we pray to God only when things are bad it means that the God we believe in is only worth our attention when things are bad. Likewise, diligence in going to God is seeking God even when things are good. God will encourage us in bad times. In good times, God will help us to keep our blessings.

Fourth, we are often reserved in our approach to God. It appears that we are more comfortable with people rather than God because we can't see Him. The bottom line is that frequently we seek human intervention to our problems without regard to God's assistance. For example, when we go to a medical doctor because we are sick, we expect to be helped even though we realize that in spite of his or her training and experience, the person is human and capable of making mistakes. Seeking medical help when we are sick is of course the correct thing to do. However, if we truly believe that God is infallible, we should trust that He can work through medical people, as well as medications and even beyond science.

Fifth, we sometimes go to God timid and tentative as "poor things." We go to God with an attitude of penitence at times when we should approach Him with a posture of privilege. Scriptures such as Micah 7:18, I John 5:3 and John 15:6 show us that it is important to go to God praying for forgiveness when we sin. Nevertheless, after we have asked forgiveness for our sins and for those who sinned against us, *we have the right as children of God to ask boldly for what we need* (see Hebrews 4:16).

• **Meditation**

Anyway, the story of Enoch gives us a sense that his special relationship with God involved more than prayers. I suspect that to enhance his prayer life, Enoch spent much time with God in seclusion and quiet periods of meditation. I doubt that the average Christian spends enough time in meditation with God. Psalm 1:1-2 says,

> *Blessed is the person who walks not in the counsel of the ungodly, nor stands in the way of sinners, nor sits in the seat of the scornful. But his or her delight is in the law of the Lord and in His law he or she meditates day and night.*

In Mark 9:29, when Jesus spoke about the power of prayer and fasting to cast out spirits, "fasting" would have included meditation. Actually, it is hard to think about Jesus praying without meditating. The Bible shows us several occasions when He sought secluded places to pray. Examples of this are found in Mark 6:46 and Mark 14:32. Certainly, the power of Jesus' ministry involved meditation.

• Role Modeling

In some ways, Enoch was a type of Christ. For instance, he did not experience death in the ordinary way. The Scripture says, "And Enoch walked with God: and he was not; for God took him" (Genesis 5:24). He is also typical of everyone who is going to heaven.

> Behold, I show you a mystery; we shall not all sleep, but we shall all be changed. In a moment, in the twinkling of an eye, at the last trump, for the trumpet shall sound, and the dead shall be raised

incorruptible, and we shall be changed. For this corruptible must put on incor-ruption, and this mortal must put on immortality. So when this corruptible shall have put on incorruption, and this mortal shall have put on immortality, then shall be brought to pass the saying that is written, "Death is swallowed up in victory. O death, where is thy sting? O grave, where is thy victory?" I Corinthi-ans 15:51-55

Through his life of testimony, Enoch en-couraged us to live for God. At the same time, Enoch prophesied against those who lived otherwise.

And Enoch also, the seventh from Adam, prophesied of these, saying, "Watch, the Lord comes with ten thou-sands of his saints to execute judg-ment upon all, and to convince all who are ungodly among them of all their ungodly deeds which they have un-godly committed, and of all their hard speeches which ungodly sinners have spoken against Him." Jude 1:14-15

Enoch was a role model for God and an example for us because he typified Christ and the saints. Like Jesus and Enoch, our lives should blend so much with the will of God that it becomes clear to others that we belong to God. When our lives attest to the existence of God, we comply with an important reason why we should be role models for God. Since no one has seen God, *it pleases God to have people as role models for Him.*

We often speak of the importance of good role models for children. We believe that this can be helpful for them to become successful adults. As Christians growing in our belief and faith, we also need role models. Observing other Christians as role models for God helps us to mature spiritually and to live successfully for God.

Principles of Belief and Practices of Faith

We live in a time of great fear and anxiety relating to nuclear and biological warfare among other things. Still, we can live without trepidation and apprehension by living successfully based on the model of Enoch. That is, to spend quality time in prayer, reflection, devotion, and meditation with God.

PRINCIPLE AND PRACTICE THREE
Being the Exception

By faith Noah, being warned of God of things not seen as yet, moved with fear, prepared an ark to save his family; by which he condemned the world, and became heir of the righteousness which is by faith. Hebrews 11:7

The statement about Noah in Hebrews 11:7 is referring to an account in Genesis 6:9-9:18. Noah lived an upright life in fellowship with God. The definitive statement about Noah is found in Genesis 6:9. "Noah was a just man and perfect in his generations, and Noah walked with God."

• **Walking for God**

Instead of the expression "walked with God," for the purpose of this principle of belief and practice of faith, I chose the term "walking for God" because Noah was an exception in a world of evil and violent people.

Ultimately, God decided to send a flood on earth for forty days and nights to destroy all the people except Noah and his family. For that reason, Noah's walk for God was in a sense dying for God. This conforms to a figurative use of the Hebrew word "walk" meaning to die. Noah more than survived the flood; he was "reborn" to a new life with God.

We can find two things that underscore Noah's walking for God in Genesis 6:9.

1. Noah was a just man.

The term "Noah was just" means that he had the right attitude toward God. He was obedient to God. As Habakkuk 2:4 states, "See, his soul which is lifted up is not upright in him but the just shall live by his faith." Noah did not hesitate to follow God's instructions in the face of ridicule from his contemporaries. As Hebrews 10:38 states, "Now the just shall live by faith but if any person drawback, My soul shall have no pleasure in him."

2. Noah was a perfect man.

The expression "Noah was perfect" means that he was sound and mature. As we grow in faith, we seek maturity in Christ. Ephesians 4:13-15 states,

> *Until we all come in the unity of the faith, and of the knowledge of the Son of God, to a perfect person, to the measure of the stature of the fullness of Christ. That we henceforth be no more children, tossed to and fro, and carried about with every wind of doctrine, by the cunningness of people, and tricky craftiness, whereby they lie in wait to deceive. But speaking the truth in love,*

may grow up into Him in all things,
which is the Head, even Christ.

There are three elements of God's actions in the story of Noah that are important relative to us living an exceptional life for God. God *designates, separates, and regenerates.*

• **God Designates**

In the process of saving Noah and his family, God made at least three significant designations.

1. *God designated Noah to build an ark according to His specifications (Genesis 6:14-16).*
2. *God's contract with Noah designated that he, his wife, his three sons and their wives, enter the ark seven days before the flood (Genesis 6:18).*
3. *God also designated that a male and female of all living things go into the ark along with sufficient food (Genesis 6:19-21).*

Being the Exception

When we walk for God, He designates what we need to handle the critical areas of our lives.

• **God Separates**

God shut the door behind Noah!

And they who went in, male and female of all flesh, as God had commanded Noah and the Lord shut him in.
Genesis 7:16

There are times when God separates us from evil. A case in point is that God separated Lot and his family from Sodom and Gomorrah before He destroyed the cities (see Genesis 19:12-26).

Furthermore, God constantly gives us time before He executes judgment. Without a doubt, "The Lord is merciful and gracious, slow to anger, and plenteous in mercy. He will not always chide neither will He keep His anger forever" (Psalm 103:8-9).

• **God Regenerates**

After the flood, Noah continued his devotion to God by sacrificing clean animals to Him. God responded by making two promises to Noah.

The first promise indicates a typing between Adam and the Creation Story with Noah and God's regeneration of the earth.

Domination and Procreation

Adam and Domination

God said, "Let us make humans in Our image, after Our likeness: and let them have dominion over the fish of the sea, and over the fowl of the air, and over the cattle, and over all the earth, and over every creeping thing that creeps on the earth." So God created human in His own image, in the image of God created He them; male and female created He them. God blessed them, and God said to them, "Be fruitful, and multiply, and replenish the earth, and subdue it; and have dominion over the fish of the sea, and over the fowl of the air, and over every living thing that moves on the earth." Then God said, "Watch, I have given you every herb bearing seed which is on the face of all the earth and every tree, which is the fruit of a tree yielding seed; to you they shall be food. And to every animal of the earth, and to every fowl of the air, and to everything that creeps on earth, wherein there is life, I have given every green herb for food;" and it was so. Genesis 1:26-30

Noah and Procreation

God blessed Noah and his sons, and said to them, "Be fruitful, and multiply, and replenish the earth. The fear of you and the dread of you shall be upon every animal of the earth, and upon every fowl of the air, upon all that move upon the earth, and upon all the fishes of the sea; into your hand are they delivered. Every moving thing that lives shall be food for you; even as the green herb have I given you all things." Genesis 9:1-3

The second promise indicates a typing between Adam and the salvation of humans and Noah and the redemption of humans.

Salvation and Redemption

Adam and Salvation

The Lord God said to the serpent, "Because you have done this, you are cursed above all cattle, and above every animal of the field; upon thy belly shall you go, and dust shall you eat all the days of your life. I will put enmity between you and the woman, and between your descendants and her descendants; it shall bruise your head, and you shall bruise his heel." Genesis 3:14-15

This passage of scripture is generally taken to mean that eventually Jesus will be victorious over all evils.

Noah and Redemption

Although the imagination of human's heart is evil from their youth, for human's sake I will not curse the earth anymore, neither will I afflict any more everything that lives. Genesis 8:20-21

• Signs

Signs are central to Noah's story. Before the flood the ark itself was a sign of things to come even though there was no sign of rain. After the flood, the rainbow became a sign of a promise to Noah. God promised never again to destroy all life on earth by water.

I will establish my covenant with you. Never again shall all people be cut off by the waters of a flood; neither shall there anymore be a flood to destroy the earth. God said, "This is the token of the covenant which I make between me and you and every living creature that is with you, for perpetual generations. I set my bow in the cloud, and it shall be for a token of a covenant between me and the earth." Genesis 9:11-14

There were no atmospheric water and presumably rain clouds before the flood. So, it is interesting that the rainbow is an arch of colors made up of sunlight and water droplets in the atmosphere. It is a symbol of the times before and after the flood. The fact is that God didn't promise to restore a rainless time. The new deal included rain!

Challenges are not always completely removed when we pass through the floods of life. At times, the residues of our past troubles remain. We see a typology of this from the life of Jacob. Jacob's hip was put out of the joint when he wrestled with an angel (see Genesis 32:25). This served as a permanent reminder to him that once he was Jacob (a trickster) who became Israel (a prince of God).

• **Witnessing**

Hebrews 11:7 says that Noah "moved with fear." In a broad sense, Noah witnessed through faith by "moving in fear." Nevertheless, there are distinctions in the witnessing of Abel, Enoch, and Noah. Comparing these distinctions gives us a clearer understanding of what is really witnessing for God.

- Abel was a *witness* for God ***through his giving.***

- Enoch spent a lifetime *witnessing* ***through his faithfulness to God.***

- Noah *witnessed* for God by **preparing for the unknown.**

Habitually, we use the words "testimony" and "witness" interchangeably in Christian talk. They both have some of the same essential meanings including evidence and attesting to firsthand accounts.

But in Noah's example of being an exception for God, there is a vital difference between testimony and witness. In the case of Enoch, his testimony for God was based on known facts. In contrast, Noah witnessed about something that he had not seen.

What Noah had never seen was rain. No one had seen rain before for that matter. At any rate, they had never seen water pouring from the sky causing floods. Hence, Noah built the ark because of the "evidence of unseen things."

Generally, our witness is based on what we *believe* is true. Central to the Principle of Belief and Practice of Faith of Being the Exception is that Noah's witnessing was not based on people's doubts but on his confidence of what no one had seen or experienced. According to Hebrews 11:1, through faith we can know what we have not experienced.

We can assume that people believed that Noah was crazy. It appears that people felt the same way about biblical people of faith who witnessed to what they had not seen. Here are two examples. In the Old Testament, it is evident from the reaction of Elijah's servant that he thought that it was incredulous when the prophet predicted much rain without clouds (see I kings 18:41-46). In the New Testament, Paul was called "mad" for preaching Jesus who he had never actually seen but had studied *the way* of Christ and became totally convicted of His truth (see Acts 26:1-25).

Many believers are called crazy for their witnessing because they see what others cannot see. The challenge for many of us is to believe strongly enough in what we pray for, so that we can actually see it spiritually before it is manifested. That in itself motivates us to act on our belief.

Principles of Belief and Practices of Faith

It's easy to say that we believe. It's hard to act on our belief when it seems crazy. If the sun was shining brightly and God told you that it was going to rain, believing God would you go into the streets with a raincoat, a rain hat, and boots?

Witnessing is always more than talk. Like Abel and Enoch, Noah's actions spoke as much as his words.

- Abel practiced his faith by *giving his best to God.*

- Enoch practiced his faith by *living a life that testified about God.*

- Noah practiced his faith by *doing something exceptional for God.*

We have never seen Jesus but we believe that he died to save us. Because of this, like Noah, there are times when we witness that we must take a stand for what we believe without necessarily seeing it.

• **Disobedience and Belief**

The opposite of witnessing is disobedience. In regard to witnessing, disobedience is ignoring what God tells us to do or acting contrary to what we believe He is telling us to do.

Disobedience diminishes faith because it doesn't get us beyond our disbelief. In Mark 9:24, the father who wanted Jesus to heal his sick child, "cried out, and said with tears, Lord, I believe; help my unbelief."

• **Warnings and Belief**

By faith Noah, being warned of God of things not seen as yet, moved with fear. Hebrews 11:7

Warning is an important component of belief and faith. Noah believed God's warnings. In the Old Testament, particularly through the prophets, God gave lots of warnings to people before He inflicted judgment on them. For example, God warned the people through

Isaiah before they were attacked by foreign countries.

The Lord said, "Wash you, make you clean, put away the evil of your doings from before my eyes; cease to do evil, learn to do well, seek judgment, relieve the oppressed, judge the fatherless, plead for the widow. Come now, and let us reason together, though your sins be as scarlet, they shall be as white as snow; though they be red like crimson, they shall be as wool. If you are willing and obedient, you shall eat the good of the land. But if you refuse and rebel, you shall be devoured with the sword, for the mouth of the Lord has spoken it." Isaiah 1:16-20

In the New Testament, Jesus gave warnings based on Old Testament incidents. For instance, Jesus warned that as in Noah and Lot's times, life would go on as usual until He suddenly returns to execute judgment.

Being the Exception

As it was in the days of Noe, so shall it be also in the days of the Son of Man. They did eat, they drank, they married wives, they were given in marriage, until the day that Noe entered into the ark, and the flood came, and destroyed them all. Likewise also as it was in the days of Lot; they did eat, they drank, they bought, they sold, they planted, they built; but the same day that Lot went out of Sodom it rained fire and brimstone from heaven, and destroyed them all. Even thus shall it be in the day when the Son of Man is revealed. Luke 17:26-30

The point is, unless we believe God's warning we will not act in faith.

• Salvation and Faith

Noah prepared an ark to save of his house. Hebrews 11:7

After believing God, by faith Noah built an ark that saved him and his family. It was not just what Noah did that saved him. It was also why he did it that saved him. He did it that he and his family might be saved.

> *For by grace you are saved through faith, and not of yourselves; it is the gift of God, not of works, in case any person should boast. Ephesians 2:8-9*

Noah was not working for salvation. He believed God and responded by building an ark. The people did not believe God so they did not respond. We cannot work for our salvation. However, without a response we cannot be saved. *A salvation response is always a faith response.* Of course, the response that saves us is to believe in Jesus Christ and accept Him as our Lord and Savior.

• Condemnation and Faith

By which he condemned the world. Hebrews 11:7

Noah's faith condemned the unbelievers. We condemn ourselves through disobedience when we act contrary to God's instructions. This condemnation comes from not believing God and not having faith to follow His instructions.

• Righteousness and Faith

And became heir of the righteousness which is by faith. Hebrews 11:7

There is no question that we are rewarded because of our faith. The greatest reward is to be made right with God.

Principles of Belief and Practices of Faith

The Lord said to Noah, "Come you and all those in your family into the ark; for I have seen that you are righteous before me among this people."
Genesis 7:1

Noah was not good enough to be saved. So, God accepted Noah's faith responses as righteousness. We too are not good enough to be saved. As a matter of fact, no one has ever been good enough to be saved and no one will ever be good enough to be saved. We are saved through what God counts as righteousness based on our faith. Again, for us this is to accept Jesus as our savior.

Like Noah, we should live exceptionally for God. However, there are three important experiences of belief and faith that we must go through as exceptional people for God in order to live successfully. The first is to understand the *In the Meanwhile* of God. The second is to practice the *Straightway* of God. The third is to realize the *Favors* of God.

• **The In the Meanwhile of Belief and Faith**

They for some time were disobedi-ent, however, the patience of God was evident in the days of Noah, while the ark was being prepared, wherein only eight people were saved from the flood.
1 Peter 3:20

After asking God to bless us, the *In the Mean-while* of faith is the period we go through while waiting on His response. At times, we stop believing that God is going to act so we stop waiting. Here are two scriptures telling us why we should wait.

The first is Isaiah 40:28-31.

Do you not know? Have you not heard that the everlasting God, the Lord, the Creator of the ends of the earth, does not grow weak, neither is weary? There is no limit to His understanding.

117

He gives power to the weak; and to them who have no might He increases their strength. Even the youths shall grow weak and be weary, and the young men shall utterly fall, but they who wait on the Lord shall renew their strength; they shall mount up with wings as eagles; they shall run, and not be weary; and they shall walk, and not grow weak.

The second is Psalm 27:14.

Wait on the Lord, be of good courage, and He shall strengthen your heart; wait, I say, on the Lord.

The Hebrew word for "wait" in the two passages above means more to *hope* and *trust* than it means to wait in the regular sense. However, when Christians quote these scriptures, generally, we understand these scriptures to mean simply "to wait." In fact, we often wait and do nothing! While we wait, we must plan for our blessings. In the final analysis, why wait on something or somebody who we do not trust?

Sometimes, God does extraordinary things while we wait. When a ruler of a synagogue came to Jesus to cure his sick daughter, Jesus was delayed on the way to his house. In the meanwhile, He healed a woman who was chronically ill. In the meanwhile also the little girl died. Jesus then went to the house and brought her back to life. The woman had been sick for twelve years. The girl was twelve years old (see Mark 5:21-43). Were the length of the woman's illness and the age of the little girl a coincidence or a sign in the narrative?

Nevertheless, there are times that while we are waiting to be blessed, God is giving us signs. At times these messages are subtle. We should pay attention to small events in our lives. The seemingly meaningless things in our lives often are connected. We should take these things as signs from God and be ready to move without delay. Here is an example from the Scripture.

Elijah said to Ahab, "Get up, eat and drink, for there is a sound of abundance of rain." So Ahab went up to eat and to drink. Elijah went up to the top of Mount Carmel and he cast himself down on the earth, and put his face between his knees, and said to his servant, "Go up now, look toward the sea." He went up, looked, and said, "There is nothing." Elijah said, "Go again seven times." And it came to pass at the seventh time that the servant said, "Take a look, there is a little cloud arising out of the sea, like a man's hand." Then Elijah said, "Go up, tell Ahab, prepare your chariot and you get down so that the rain does not stop you." I Kings 18:41-44

As I previously stated, Elijah's predicted a lot of rain without clouds. When the first cloud as small as a man's hand appeared, Elijah was certain that *in the meanwhile* heavy rain was coming. He connected the seemingly insignificant thing as a small cloud with torrential rain. Verse 45 of the passage of scripture actually contains the words "in the meanwhile."

> Then **in the meanwhile** it came to pass that the heaven became black with clouds and wind, and there was a great rain. I Kings 18:45

By the way, Noah did not wait to see rain drops before he acted in faith. And, God was not waiting for Noah to build the ark; He was waiting for people to get right.

• **The Straightway of Belief and Faith**

If God has not acted on particular issues in the past does not mean that He will not act on them in the present or in the future. It does not mean either that when God acts He will not act swiftly and completely. Jesus Himself compares His second coming to the swiftness of how God eventually acted in the time of Noah.

> *But as the days of Noe were, so shall also the coming of the Son of Man be. For as in the days that were before the flood they were eating and drinking, marrying and giving in marriage, until the day that Noe entered the ark, and did not know that the flood was coming that took them all away; so shall also the coming of the Son of Man be. Matthew 24:37-39*

As in Noah's time, the *straightway* of faith is not dependent on our time but God's time. We must believe God and act in our time because certainly God will act in His own time.

Again, I refer to the narrative in Mark 5:25-34. A woman with constant bleeding that had worsened over twelve years and had exhausted her finances on medical resources pressed through a large crowd and touched

Jesus' clothes. She believed that by doing this she would be cured. She "felt in her body that she was healed" (Mark 5:29). The word "felt" actually means *knew*. She was healed "straightway" (Mark 5:29) and knew immediately. This correlates to the fact that Jesus also *knew* that healing power had gone out from Him (see Mark 5:30).

Luke 8:44 indicates that it was the "border" of his garment that she "touched." Broad stripes of colored cloths were used on the borders of men's outer garments (Numbers 15:38; Matthew 23:5). Since this portion of a man's garment depicted his importance in society, it is very plausible that the woman touched the blue striped border of Jesus' garment acknowledging that He was from the royal line of King David and that He was the Messiah. This conviction of who Jesus was moved her *immediately* to draw from His healing power. Once we are convinced that God will move on situations in our lives we must *straightway* put ourselves in the positions to receive His blessings.

• **The Favors of Belief and Faith**

But Noah found grace in the eyes of the Lord. Genesis 6:8

The word "grace" in the above verse also means *favor.* I use the word favor in this book to mean an explicit pattern of God's blessing. In terms of belief and faith, God gives us four favors. They are mercy, grace, kindness, and goodness.

1. *Mercy* This is what God gives us instead of giving us what *we deserve.* In other words, He gives us nothing when we deserve something. For instance, when we are disobedient and He does not punish us, this is His mercy. So, God is merciful to us just by doing nothing to us! Furthermore, if we are punished, whatever discipline that He may give us is always less than we deserve, so He is still merciful. That is why the Scripture says; "Let them now that fear the Lord say that his mercy endures forever" (Psalm 118:4).

Being the Exception

I suspect that believers do not draw on the power of God's mercy enough. First of all, I think that when we are disobedient to God we often don't ask God for mercy. Moreover, frequently when we ask for God's mercy, we simultaneously ask Him to fix things. This attitude is hardly being contrite, penitent, and repentant.

For this reason, Jesus spoke parables against unforgiving and merciless folks. Matthew 18:23-35 relate that a servant after pleading with his lord to have patience was forgiven of his debts. The same servant went out and met someone who owed him less money than his lord had forgiven him. The person begged for time to repay but the pleas were ignored. Instead of being forgiven the person was sent to prison. When the lord heard of this he called the servant and said,

"You wicked servant, I forgave all your debts because you asked me; should you not also have compassion on your

fellow servant, even as I had pity on you?" Matthew 18:32-33

Jesus added:

"His lord was extremely angry and delivered him to the tormentors, until he should pay all that was due to him. So likewise shall My heavenly Father do also to you if you from your hearts do not forgive everyone their trespasses." Matthew 18:34-35

Jesus also made it clear that the more we are favored by God's mercy is the more mercy we should be willing to show others. There are no thought and feeling more powerful than when we realize that we are blessed because of mercy.

But the person who did not know and committed things worthy of stripes, shall be beaten with few stripes. For to whomsoever much is given, of

126

that person shall be much required.
Luke 12:48

2. *Grace* This is what God gives us that we *do not deserve*. It's unmerited or unearned favor from God. Because of God's mercy, grace is given to us in place of punishment. "For the wages of sin is death; but the gift of God is eternal life through Jesus Christ our Lord" (Romans 6:23). Here the word "gift" can be interpreted as grace. They are both related to receiving something free. Therefore, Noah believed God and received grace not mercy.

We regularly use the words mercy and grace interchangeably. Just the same, at times the Bible indicates a distinction between these words.

Mercy at times is connected to the unbeliever.

I thank Christ Jesus our Lord, Who has enabled me, because He counted me faithful, putting me into the ministry. Previously, I was a blasphemer, a persecutor, and injurious, but I obtained mercy, because I did it igno-rantly in unbelief. I Timothy 1:12-13

Grace sometimes is more related to the believer.

Grow in grace and in the knowledge of our Lord and Savior Jesus Christ. 2 Peter 3:18

What this means is that for believers, God's inclination is to move from mercy to grace. Paul relates this from God to us this way:

He said to me, "My grace is sufficient for you because my strength is made perfect in weakness." Most gladly therefore will I rather glory in my infir-mities so that the power of Christ may rest on me. 2 Corinthians 12:9

3. *Kindness* This is God's act of allowing us to use the blessings that He gives us. For in-

stance, God blessed Noah to build an ark to save him and his family. Subsequently, God personally took care of them for at least 371 days while they were in the ark (see Genesis 7:1-8:19). The ark would be of no use if they could not survive in it. As Christians, God allows us to use His blessings through Jesus Christ.

> *And has raised us up together, and made us sit together in heavenly places in Christ Jesus so that in the ages to come He might show the exceeding riches of His grace by His kindness toward us through Christ Jesus. Ephesians 2:6-7*

4. *Goodness* This is God's way of allowing us to use His blessings over and over. It was not that Noah was good enough for God but God was always good for Noah. He was blessed even to the point that God did not permit him to leave the boat until it was safe (Genesis 8:6-12).

King David knew that God is good all the time and all the time God is good. David said that he fully expected to be blessed repeatedly by God.

> *I would have given up if I had not believed that I would see the goodness of the Lord in the land of the living.*
> ***Psalm 27:13***

• **Being the Exception for God**

We are exceptions for God when we walk for Him and not allow ourselves to be influenced by what unbelievers think of Him. Besides, many unbelievers think that evil is "powerful" and God is "powerless." Nevertheless, we must make them see the power of God through our belief and faith in Him.

The essence of our witness is what we believe, not just what we know or what we have experienced. We must believe that God has the power to move, change, and transform situations and conditions regardless of the time it takes and we should be prepared to act according to those convictions.

PRINCIPLE AND PRACTICE FOUR
Following the Vision

By faith Abraham, when he was called to go out into a place which later he received as an inheritance, obeyed, and he went out, not knowing where he went. By faith he sojourned in the land of promise, as in a strange country, dwelling in tabernacles with Isaac and Jacob, the heirs with him of the same promise as he looked for a city which had foundations, whose Builder and Maker is God. Hebrews 11:8-10

Hebrews 11:8-10 is referring to Genesis 12:1 where Abram (later called Abraham) at seventy five years old was directed by God to take his family to a land unknown to them. They literally walked to a land that God showed them. Once again, God was separating believers from the environment of evil people (see Joshua 24:2-3).

• **Waking by Faith**

God promised Abraham tremendous blessings if he would "walk by faith." Abraham obeyed. As a result, all believers are blessed through Abraham.

> *I will make of you a great nation, and I will bless you, and make your name great and you shall be a blessing to all. I will bless them who bless you, and curse them who curse you. In you shall all families of the earth be blessed. Genesis 12:2-3*

There are several ways to express "walking" as it relates to faith. Here are three:

- Enoch *walked with God by faith*. His worship was his **testimony**.

- Noah *walked for God by faith*. He witnessed through **fellowship**.

Following the Vision

- Abraham *walked by faith for God.* He exhibited **followship**. I coined this verb sounding word "followship" from the noun fellowship.

In a general way, we get a sense of an Old Testament meaning of "walk" here. That is, "to walk about." As Abraham moved from place to place following God's instructions, he continued to develop in faith. First, Abraham moved from one part to another part of Mesopotamia (Acts 7:2-4). Then, he moved from present day Iraq to present day Palestine and Israel after wandering for a period of at least ten years (Genesis 12:4-9). Later, he moved from this area to Egypt and back (Genesis 12:10-13:1). Eventually, he separated from his nephew Lot and was nomadic in the hill country of Palestine for at least fifteen years (Genesis 13:8-18). Finally, he sojourned in southern Canaan (Genesis 20:1). As Abraham walked by faith, he became increasingly successful. Most of all, he became a successful person in God's eyes.

Principles of Belief and Practices of Faith

It is important to note that in Abraham's walk by faith for God, each trial he encountered resulted in triumph. Here are some examples:

a. *Trial* Abraham left Mesopotamia which was a fertile region to go to Palestine, a country with many rocky regions (Genesis 12:5).
Triumph Abraham became a successful herdsman (Genesis 13:1).

b. *Trial* Abraham went from apparently a comfortable living in Iraq to living in tents as a nomad in Canaan (Genesis 12:1; Hebrews 11: 9).
Triumph Abraham became the father of a large nation (Genesis 12:7).

c. *Trial* Abraham had to flee to Egypt because the land that God promised him became a place of great famine (Genesis 12:10).

Triumph Abraham left Egypt a rich man (Genesis 13:1-2).

d. *Trial* Abraham got the worse part of the grazing land when Lot parted with him (Genesis 13: 7-10).
Triumph After Lot left, Abraham was compensated when God gave him and his descendants forever all the land that he could see where he stood (Genesis 13:14-17).

• **Walking by Faith and not by Sight**

Certainly, God directed Abraham experiences. In this context I think of God as "ordering Abraham's steps." I draw this from Psalm 119:133 that says, "Order my steps in Your word and let not any iniquity have dominion over me." In other words, God "kept him from stumbling" as he walked by faith and not by sight. Hence, we can conclude that there were times when Abraham "didn't know where he was going." This conforms to 2 Corinthians 5:7, "For we walk by faith, not by sight." Regarding this, I draw from an imagery found in Proverbs 3:5-7.

> *Trust in the Lord with all your heart, and lean not to your own understanding. In all your ways acknowledge Him, and He shall direct your paths. Be not wise in your own eyes but fear the Lord and depart from evil.*

We tend to trust in what we "know" as absolute truths even though our knowledge of many things keep changing all the time. People once believed that the earth was flat! Scientists had to modify the Laws of Gravity because of the Theory of Relativity. Now, it seems likely that the Theory of Relativity will be modified because of new discoveries suggesting that matter can travel faster than the speed of light. Since we shouldn't lean on our understanding, we should let God direct our path.

Given that faith is acting on what we believe before we see the results, in that case, we walk by faith and not by sight. In other words, when we walk by faith we are walking blindly. I use the metaphor of blindness based on the scripture 2 Corinthians 5:7 that I mentioned previously. While this isn't flattering, it brings the point home.

Now, in terms of this principle of belief and practice of faith, walking blindly by faith is not walking by "blind faith." Faith actions are deliberate and are directed by God. So, walking blindly by faith is depending on God. On the other hand, blind faith suggests accidents and coincidences.

As we walk blindly, the walking stick that we "lean" on is our belief in the power of God. This is how we trust God, we lean on Him. What is more, we can depend on God to watch out for us.

The Lord is my shepherd, I shall not want. He makes me lie down in green pastures; He leads me beside the still waters, He restores my soul, He leads me in the paths of righteousness for His name's sake. Psalm 23:1-3

A shepherd, of course, totally cares for the sheep. There were at least three important functions of the shepherd's staff relative to the care of the sheep. First, the shepherd used the curved part of the staff to *guide* strayed sheep gently back to the fold. Second, the shepherd used the rod of the staff to *protect* the flock from wild animals. Third, the shepherd watching the sheep for many hours while standing would likely lean on the staff for *support.*

Although I walk through the valley of the shadow of death, I will fear no evil, for You are with me; Your rod and Your staff they comfort me. Psalm 23:4

As believers and priests of God, we can depend on His support as we walk by faith. In fact, God promised us tremendous blessings when we are faithful to Him in our walk.

> *I will raise Me up a faithful priest that shall do according to that which is in My heart and in My mind, and I will build for him or her a sure house; and he or she shall walk before My anointed forever. 1Samuel 2:35*

Fellowship, discipleship, and stewardship are three words that Christians often use to describe their walk with God.

• *Fellowship*

A *Fellowship* is an association in which people have certain things in common. Sometimes "to fellowship" simply means people "getting together." The Christian fellowship is a partnership based on our common beliefs and practices of faith. However, for a person to be "in fellowship" does not always mean that he or she is *committed* to the group. Commonly, when people commit themselves in a fellowship they do so in various degrees. For instance, in many churches members set their own standards of commitment instead of complying with the spirit of the fellowship. In the Early Church, there were the incidents of Ananias and Sapphira.

> *A certain man named Ananias, with Sapphira his wife, sold a possession, and kept back part of the price, his wife also being privy to it, and brought a certain part, and laid it at the apostles' feet. But Peter said, "Ananias, why has satan filled your heart to lie to the Holy Ghost, and to keep back part of the price of the land? While it remained, was it not your own? And after it was sold, was it not in your own power? Why have you conceived this thing in your heart? You have not lied to human beings, but to God." Ana-*

nias hearing these words fell down and died; and great fear came on all the people who heard these things. Then the young men arose, wrapped him up and carried him out, and buried him. After that, it was about the space of three hours when his wife, not knowing what was done, came in. Peter said to her, "Tell me whether you sold the land for the amount you brought." She responded, "Yes, for that much." Then Peter said to her, "How is it that you have agreed together to tempt the Spirit of the Lord? Behold, the feet of them who have buried your husband are at the door, and shall carry you out." She fell down immediately at his feet, and died. The young men came in and saw her. They carried her out and buried her by her husband. Great fear came on all the church and on many who heard these things. Acts 5:1-11.

• **Discipleship**

Generally, *discipleship* is following a leader or specific beliefs. The word disciple is distinctively derived from a word meaning, "to learn." In terms of Christianity, discipleship is for the particular purpose of learning about Jesus. However, disciples are not always *loyal* to their teachers or teachings.

> *A certain ruler asked Jesus, "Good Master, what shall I do to inherit eternal life?" Jesus said to him, "Why do you call me good? Nobody is good, except One. He is God. You know the commandments: Do not commit adultery, do not kill, do not steal, do not bear false witness, honor your father and your mother." The ruler responded, "All these commandments I have kept from my youth." Now when Jesus heard these things, He told him, "Yet, you lack one thing; sell all that you have and distribute it to the poor,*

and you shall have treasure in heaven, and come, follow Me." When he heard this, he was very sorrowful because he was very rich. Luke 18:18-23

This ruler essentially began his discipleship with Jesus when he sought to learn from Him. In spite of his eagerness to learn from Jesus, he could not "follow" because he was more loyal to his wealth.

• **Stewardship**

Stewardship is managing another person's property trustworthily. Christians are trustees of God's blessings to them. Nevertheless, stewards are not always responsible people.

The kingdom of heaven is as a man travelling into a far country who called his own servants, and delivered to them his goods. To one he gave a portion of money of five talents, to another two, and to another one; to each man according to his investment ability. Then he left immediately. He who received the portion of money of five talents went and traded with the same and gained five more talents. Likewise he who received two also gained another two. But he who received one went and dug in the earth and hid his lord's money. After a long time the lord of those servants came and settled his investment accounts with them. So, he who had received the portion of money of five talents came and brought the other five talents, saying, "Lord, you gave me five talents, look, I have gained five talents more." His lord said to him, "Well done, you good and faithful servant, you have been faithful over a few things, I will make you ruler over many things. Enter into the joy of your lord." He also who had received two talents came and said, "Lord, you gave me two talents, look, I have gained two other talents." His lord said to him, "Well done you good and faithful servant you have been faithful over a few things, I will make you ruler over many things. Enter into the joy of your lord." Then he who had received the one talent came and said, "Lord, I knew that you are a hard man, reaping where you have not sown, and gathering where you have not scattered seeds. I was afraid, and went and hid your money in the earth. Look, here is your money." His lord spoke to him, "You wicked and lazy servant, you knew that I reap where I do not sow, and gather where I do not scatter seeds; therefore you should have invested my money with the exchangers, and then at my coming I would have received my interest. Take therefore the talent from him, and give it to him who has ten talents. For everyone who has, more shall be given, but from them who have not shall be taken away even that which they have. Cast the unprofitable servant into outer darkness where there shall be weeping and grinding of teeth." Matthew 25:14-30

We know too well that stewardship for some people means holding on to God's blessing and not sharing with others. There are many Christian groups who never reach their full potential because they don't invest their blessings. For example, members of many churches tend to buy the cheapest of everything they can find for the church, even the cheapest foods. The results are that we repeatedly buy the same things because they do not last, and sometimes trying to economize, the types of foods we buy for church functions are not the healthiest.

• Followship

Followship is a word that I use to mean something that goes beyond fellowship, discipleship, and stewardship to include *following*

Following the Vision

Jesus with *commitment*, *loyalty*, and *responsibility*. Luke 9:57-62 gives us three illustrations that bring out vital elements of followship as opposed to fellowship, discipleship, and stewardship.

> *It came to pass, that, as they went in the way, a certain man said to him, "Lord, I will follow you wherever you go." Jesus said to him, "Foxes have holes, and birds of the air have nests but the Son of Man has nowhere to lay His head." Luke 9:57-58*

In the above passage, a person volunteered to follow Jesus. Jesus stated that He was a homeless person. Based on Jesus' response, we can assume that this person did not make a *commitment* to follow Jesus.

> *Jesus said to another, "Follow Me." But he said, "Lord, allow me first to go and bury my father." Jesus told him, "Let the dead bury their dead but go*

and preach the kingdom of God." Luke 9:59-60

This time Jesus invited someone to follow Him. The reply to Jesus suggests that this person didn't want to jeopardize his inheritance. Probably, he was an elder son who was required to stay at home until the death of his father. Certainly, this person's *loyalty* was to material things.

> *And another also said, "Lord, I will follow You but let me first go bid them farewell who are at home at my house." Jesus told him, "No person having put his or her hand to the plough, while looking back, is fit for the kingdom of God." Luke 9:61-62*

Again, another person wanted to follow Jesus but apparently desired to go home first possibly to seek permission of relatives. This person was not willing to take *responsibility* for his or her actions.

Following the Vision

All three illustrations have a common thread. The would-be followers sought *security* before they followed Christ.

- The *first person* sought *security* of a **place to live.**
- The *second person* sought *security* of **income.**
- The *third person* sought *security* of a **place to return.**

Moreover, the section of scripture that immediately precedes these illustrations points out five things that are the greater context of Luke 9:57-62.

1. Jesus said that He would be rejected and killed (Luke 9:22).
2. Jesus foretold His death (Luke 9:44).
3. Jesus was on His way to Jerusalem. This meant impending crucifixion for Him (Luke 9:51-53).
4. Jesus was not allowed to stay in Samaria on His way to Jerusalem (Luke 9:53).

5. Jesus objected to the disciples' request to deal with the rejection of the Samaritans by destroying them with fire (Luke 9:54).

Most likely, with knowledge of some or all the above, the would-be followers probably considered the possibility that the ministry of Jesus might not succeed. In any case, other ways of looking at these illustrations are:

a) The first person was *concerned* about **self.**
b) The second person was *concerned* about **the dead.**
c) The third person was *concerned* about **family.**

None of these *concerns* was about Jesus. Followship requires that we concern ourselves with the people with whom we share fellowship, discipleship, or stewardship.

Following the Vision

In the end, followship is not about looking back. It's focusing on the task that God has on hand for us. It's our ministry! In reality, followship often put us on a road to life's challenges.

This principle of belief and practice of faith shows us that if we walk by faith and not by what we see, God will order our steps. Like Abraham, we might encounter difficulties, but eventually we will be richly blessed. In order to achieve this we need to have a vision.

• **Vision**

Although we walk blindly we must always have a *vision*. We can look ahead in terms of what Hebrews 11:1 states, *envisioning the things hoped for.* To have a vision means that we have God's guidance. Ultimately that is why we follow Christ. We follow in Jesus' footsteps. "Where there is no <u>vision,</u> the people <u>perish</u> but the person who <u>keeps the law, happy is he or she</u>" (Proverbs 29:18).

It is important that we have a vision when we walk by faith because of at least four things in Proverbs 29:18.

1. *To perish* means to be naked. If we are naked it means that we have no plans.
2. If we have no *vision* we are without God's guidance.
3. *Keeping the law* means to trust God by his word.
4. *Happy* means to be blessed and to live successfully.

• **The Promise**

Abraham's vision was that he looked for a blessing based on the promise of God. Since we are blessed through Abraham, then we are called to walk like Abraham. In the end, walking by faith is to believe totally in what God has promised.

*Abraham is the father of believers
to them who are not believers but*

154

who also walk in the steps of that faith of our father Abraham, which is the faith he had before he believed. Romans 4:12

• **Great Expectations**

The visions from God's promises are great expectations for our lives.

- *Expect* to go to unseen places!
- *Expect* great adventures!
- *Expect* to succeed!

All of the above are parts of God's blessings when we walk by faith. So, go with confidence and trust in the promises of God's word. By the way, there is a New Testament word, *peripatein,* which means to walk. It literally denotes "to direct one's life." Incidentally, the same meaning can be a metaphor for "prosperity" or "to turn out well."

PRINCIPLE AND PRACTICE FIVE
Looking for Miracles

Also, through faith Sara herself received strength to conceive a child, and delivered the child when she was past age, because she judged Him faithful Who had made the promise. Hebrews 11:11

In Genesis 12:1-5, God instructed Abram (Abraham) to leave Mesopotamia and go to Canaan. Mesopotamia is the region in the Middle East around the Tigris and Euphrates rivers. The specific place mentioned in Genesis 11:28 where Abraham and his family lived was Ur of the Chaldees. This is still a city in present day Iraq. Canaan is in the general area of present day Israel and at least part of the country of Jordan. Often, Canaan is referred to as Palestine.

Traveling from Mesopotamia to Palestine in Abraham's time was a long and arduous journey. Presumably, this journey was made even more difficult by the fact that Abraham traveled through places that were generally occupied by people of essentially different customs than his. They were often unfriendly to foreigners who they believed intended to settle in their land. All the above factors underscore the significance of Abraham's journey of faith as it relates to the Principle of Belief and Practice of Faith of Following the Vision (see Principle and Practice Four).

• The Promise

In Genesis 12:2, before Abraham left Mesopotamia, God promised him that he would have many descendants and they would become a large nation. Genesis 12:5 records that Abraham took Sarai (Sarah) his wife with him when he left the area of today's Iraq. Genesis 12:4 states that at that time Abraham was 75 years old.

Looking for Miracles

In Genesis 13:14-17, God again made the promise to Abraham that his descendants would be many and they would possess much land. Specifically, God said to Abraham:

> *"Lift up now your eyes. Look from the place where you are, northward, southward, eastward, and westward because all the land that you see, I will give to you and your descendants forever. I will make your descendants as the dust of the earth, so that if a person can number the dust of the earth, then, your descendants could be numbered. Arise; walk through the land in the length and breadth of it because I will give it to you."*

Then, in Genesis 15:18, God made a covenant (contract or treaty) with Abraham that his descendants would occupy an extensive area of land. God said to Abraham, "I give this land to your progeny, from the river of Egypt to the great river Euphrates."

Principles of Belief and Practices of Faith

When Abraham was 99 years old, God promised Abraham again that his heirs would inherit the same promise of blessings that He gave him. This promise was actually a covenant that bound Abraham to live righteously for God. Also, Abraham's descendants would have to live righteously for God for the contract to be valid for them.

When Abram was ninety-nine years old, the Lord appeared to him and said, "I am the Almighty God, walk before Me and be perfect. I will make My covenant between you and Me. I will multiply your descendants abundantly." Abram bowed his face to the ground. God talked to him saying, "As for me, look, My covenant is with you, and you shall be a father of many nations. Your name will not be Abram anymore. Your name shall be Abraham because I will make many descendants come from you. I will make nations and kings come out of you. I will establish My covenant between you, your descendants, and Me for an everlasting covenant, to be a God to you and to them. I will give you and your descendants the land where you are a stranger, all the land of Canaan, for an everlasting possession; and I will be their God." God added, "Therefore, you and your descendants shall keep my covenant." Genesis 17: 1-9

At the time of the above scripture, Sarah was eighty-nine years old. What was significant about this was that Sarah was always unable to conceive a child (see Genesis 11:30).

Subsequently, in Genesis 17:15-16, God told Abraham that Sarah would have a son with him. At that time, Abraham was100 years old and Sarah was 90 years old.

God said to Abraham, "As for Sarai your wife, you shall not call her name Sarai, but Sarah shall be her name. I will bless her and give you a son of her.

*Indeed, I will bless her, and she shall be
a mother of nations; kings of people
shall be of her." Genesis 17:15-16*

Once more, in Genesis 18:18, God promised that a great nation would come from Abraham.

*God said, "Seeing that Abraham shall
surely become a great and mighty nation and all the nations of the earth
shall be blessed in him." Genesis 18:18*

Finally, when Sarah was about 91 years old, she gave birth to a son.

• **The Promise and Faith**

When we speak of faith, we could argue that it is an attribute of God that He allows us to share with Him. Certainly, chapter eleven of Hebrews supports this. With regard to this attribute of God, the verse below reflects the very essence of all His promises. God is faithful to His promises; it's up to us to be faithful in response.

> ***Through faith,*** *also, Sara herself received strength to procreate and delivered a child when she was past age* **because she judged him faithful who made the promise to her.** *Hebrews 11:11*

• The Promise and the in the Meanwhile

The promise given to Abraham on several occasions implies that God blesses us at times in relation to the *in the meanwhile* of our belief and faith. As I stated in Principles and Practice Three, the in the meanwhile of our belief and faith is the period we go through *while* waiting for the fulfillment of what God has promised us. When I say "waiting" in this context, I mean, "trusting." Purposely, this is trusting in God for the incredible. Accordingly, Hebrews 11:11

infers that Sarah eventually trusted that God would be faithful to His promise even though it was incredible. Thus, the in the meanwhile of our belief and faith also confirms the faithfulness of God.

The fulfillment of the in the meanwhile of belief and faith of Abraham and Sarah is expressed in Hebrews 11:12.

> *Therefore from one person, Abraham, and from him who was as good as dead, came many descendants as the stars of the sky in multitude and innumerable as the sand that is by the seashore.*

• **The Promise and Hope**

All the Principles of Belief and Practices of Faith for Successful Living relate to hope. As I previously stated, the word "hope" biblically and historically meant "confidence" or "trust." We should be reciprocal with trust and confidence in God when He makes promises to us. This is an important point of the eleventh chapter of Hebrews. Indeed, that's why the chapter begins with the statement in the first verse telling us that our faith reveals our confidence in things we hope for.

Furthermore, the statements below are very indicative of the power of hope.

> These all died in faith, not having received the promises, <u>but having seen them from far,</u> were persuaded of them. They embraced the promises, and realized that they were strangers and pilgrims on the earth. Hebrews 11:13

The above verse is very moving. I'm positive that for many of us, tears sometimes come to our eyes when we realize the joy our ancestors would have to know that many good things that they believed in and prayed for, are now happening to us. My grandmother often wondered aloud if one day some family members would replace relatives who were ministers. Today, many of her descendants are ministers.

If God does not fulfill some of our promises, He will pass them on to our children, or our children's children, or even beyond them.

• **The Promise and Jesus**

"These all died in faith, not having received the promises…" (Hebrews 11:13). The full *promise* of God wasn't realized in Isaac but in Jesus. Therefore, the promise was not just for Abraham and Sarah but also for all of us. We are part of that promise because we believe in Jesus who was a descendant of Abraham through Isaac (see Matthew 1:1-16). We share the blessings of God through Abraham. Consequently, we are part of the God's covenant with Abraham. In Romans 4:1-25, Paul carefully explains the special relationship that we have with God through His promise to Abraham.

Abraham and Sarah had no idea that we would be recipients of their promise of blessings. Likewise, God blesses us at times so that others will be blessed through us, even people unknown to us. For instance, many people have changed from selfish lifestyles to very caring ones after God miraculously healed them of diseases. Certainly, we have no idea of the far-reaching touch of God's blessings.

• **The Mystery of the Promise**

Considering what I said about God's promise to us through Abraham, for believers in Jesus, the ultimate meaning of God's promise is Christ. *Jesus is the Promise.*

Typing Abraham to Jesus based on God's promises to Abraham, reveals the following prophetic *symbolic* fulfillments:

- ❑ Jesus is the Promised Messiah.
- ❑ Jesus is the Promised Great Nation of all believers.
- ❑ Jesus is the Promise of the Great Inheritance passing from believers to believers.
- ❑ Jesus is the Holy Spirit of Promise.
- ❑ Jesus gave us everlasting life, so He is the Promised Land.

167

In the meantime, we should know that God wants to fulfill all His promises to us through Jesus Christ. In order to believe God's promises, first, we should know what His promises are. God's promises are not hidden from us. They are in the Bible. There is an extraordinary amount. God has promises for everyone. In fact, the Scripture tells us that all of God's promises came together in Jesus Christ and they are *sealed* in us through the Holy Spirit. The mysterious power of God's promises is available to us through Christ. The Holy Spirit of Promise that indwells in us is a non-refundable deposit. It is a pledge and down payment (earnest) on our total inheritance of eternal life through Jesus Christ our Lord.

> *Having made known to us the* **_mystery of His will,_** *according to His good pleasure that He purposed in Himself, that in the dispensation of the* <u>fullness of times He might gather together in one all things in Christ</u>, *both which are in heaven, and which are on earth,*

even in Him. In Whom <u>also we have</u> **<u>obtained an inheritance</u>***, being pre-destinated according to the purpose of Him who works all things after the counsel of His own will, that we should be to the praise of His glory, who first trusted in Christ. In Whom you also trusted, after you heard the word of truth, the gospel of your salvation; <u>in Whom also after you believed, you were</u>* **sealed** *with that* **Holy Spirit of Promise***, which is the* **earnest** *of our* **inheritance** *until the* **redemption of the purchased possession***, to the praise of His glory. Ephesians 1:9-14*

• **The Promise Never Dies**

The eleventh chapter of Hebrews states that the people of faith died "in faith." Of course, their faith was acting on their beliefs while they were alive. Their belief and faith lived on after they died because of three elements expressed in successive verses of Scripture.

Principles of Belief and Practices of Faith

1. They that said such things declared plainly that they sought a country. Hebrews 11:14

They were just passing through. The people of faith expected more to come from their faith than what they had experienced in their lifetime. However, they did not realize the full extent of what was to come. They did not know that the full implication of their faith would relate to our faith in God through the Messiah. Nonetheless, Jesus actually came through some of the patriarchs, such as Abraham, Isaac, and Jacob (see Matthew 1:2).

I surmise that few people would dispute that we ourselves are just "passing through" while we are alive on earth. I recently returned from visiting two towns where I grew up. I lived in a new section of the first town. The other sections were old. The people in the old sections greatly desired to have homes like those of the new section. Because of governmental regulations, they knew that this would be asking for the unthinkable on the government's part. This town is rebuilt completely now with all new homes. This is a transformation that many of the former residents who are now dead had prayed for but did not live to see.

The second town was quite affluent when I lived there. This town is merged completely now with three less affluent surrounding towns. In my opinion, none of these towns have largely benefited from these changes. This is something for which no one prayed.

The point is that changes take place in our lifetimes with things that we are familiar with whether we are present or not. Moreover, they will take place even if we die. In effect, we should live by faith believing that good things will come of *all* our experiences after we "pass through."

> *2. Truly, if they had been mindful of that country where they came from they might have had opportunity to return. Hebrews 11:15*

They had gone too far to turn back. The people of faith knew that once they were committed to their journeys of faith there would be a point of no return. As they progressed in their journey, they became focused completely on God. On our faith journey, we also should become focused entirely on God through Christ. Hebrews 12:2 states how we should do this: "Look to Jesus the Author and Finisher of our faith." At times, we come to a point in our faith walks when we realize that we have gone too far to turn back. We recognize that there are challenges ahead but we continue on our journeys because we know that there are still more blessings to come.

> *3. They desired a better country, that is, a heavenly place. What is important is that God was not ashamed to be called their God because He had prepared a city for them. Hebrews 11:16*

They wanted more. The people of faith recognized the spiritual implications of their blessings that went far beyond their material success or prosperity. Jesus taught the same reality.

> *When Jesus had called the people and His disciples to Him, He said to them, "Those who will come after Me, let them deny themselves, take up their cross and follow Me. For those who will save their lives shall lose it. But those who will lose their lives for My sake and the gospel's, those people shall save their lives. For what shall it profit a person if he or she gain the whole world and lose his or her own soul? Or, what shall a person give in exchange for his or her soul?" Mark 8:34-37*

In the final analysis, belief and faith are not primarily about our blessings but about God's glory. In point of fact, God wants to brag about us. God wants to boast about us.

Now, there was a day when the sons of God came to present themselves before the Lord and satan also came with them. The Lord asked satan, "Where are you coming from?" Satan answered, "From going to and fro on earth and from walking up and down on it." Then the Lord said to satan, <u>"Have you considered My servant Job, that there is none like him on earth, a perfect and an upright man, one that fears God, and avoids evil?"</u> Job 1:6-8

As a final point, since the Promise of God never dies with the death of a person of faith, perhaps, that's one of Jesus' reasons for saying that He came that we might have an abundant life (see John 10:10). To have an abundant life is to live successfully.

• The Impossible Made Possible

Hebrews 11:1 gives the basis for the impossible becoming possible. It declares, "Now faith is the substance of things hoped for, the evidence of things not seen." This concept extends from verse one and is built on throughout the chapter.

Hence, another way of articulating Hebrews 11:1 is to say that faith is about believing and acting on things that we don't see. Then, another way of articulating Hebrews 11:2, "For by faith the elders obtained a good report," is to say that our faith actions, even the ones that seem impossible, create examples for others to follow. Therefore, the reputation of faith materializing as the impossible is also exemplary to others after we die.

With regard to procreation, Abraham and Sarah were dead. Ordinarily, at their ages we deem it impossible for humans to be fertile or capable of bringing life into the world. Therefore, the birth of Isaac can be attributed to something besides the impossible or a biological fluke - it was also faith. *Nothing happened until they acted in faith!*

Clearly, the in the meanwhile of belief and faith here for Abraham and Sarah was that

God waited until it seems impossible then He made the "impossible" possible. This is a basic understanding of the phrase "and him as good as dead" in Hebrews 11:12.

Since God is the creator of all things, and He creates from "nothing," we can understand why He used procreation in that significant instance to demonstrate His power over life and death. This is explained in Romans 4:12-18.

Abraham is the father of believers to them who are not believers but who also walk in the steps of that faith of our father Abraham, which he had before he believed. For the promise that he should be the heir of the world, was not to Abraham, or to his descendants through the law but through the righteousness of faith. If they who are of the law are heirs, faith is made void, and the promise made ineffective because the law involves anger, and where no law is, there is no transgression. Therefore, it is of faith that it might be by

176

grace; to the end the promise might be sure to all people, not to those only of the law, but to those also of the faith of Abraham, who is the father of us all (as it is written, I have made you a father of many nations) **before God Whom he believed, Who gives life to the dead, and calls those things that are not as though they were.** *Abraham, against hope believed in hope, that he might become the father of many nations, according to that which was spoken, "So shall be your descendants."*

• **Expect Miracles**

If we believe that whatever we think is impossible is possible, then we should always expect miracles. Too many believers when asked how they are doing, frequently respond in one of three ways. They are "just holding on," "trying to make it," or "hanging in there." Now, while these are probably good descriptions of their conditions at times, I often wonder how much these kinds of responses reflect attitudes that diminish their expectations of miracles. I'm not particularly impressed by people who frequently use weak expressions to describe their circumstances! Actually, I think that many people have come to *believe* that all they can expect of their existence is to survive on the fringes of life. Eventually, for some that's all they do! On the other hand, if we believe that we can do more than "endure," we are very likely to accomplish more in life.

God works miracles in our lives for at least three purposes. First, miracles remind us that God is God. Second, miracles show us that God is doing the blessings. Third, miracles remind us that God sometimes uses us only as instruments to perform the incredulous. Many accounts of miracles in the Bible have these elements. A good way to understand these purposes is to compare some particular miracle experiences of Moses to some specific ones of Elijah.

❖ Moses Experiences on Mount Horeb (Sinai)

Moses name probably means "one who draws out." In other words, he was called to be a leader. Several centuries before Elijah, Moses received his commission from God on Mount Sinai at the "burning bush" to go to Egypt and bring His people out of slavery.

> Now, Moses kept the flock of Jethro his father-in -law, the priest of Midian. Once, when Moses led the flock to the back of the desert, <u>he came to the mountain of God, **Horeb**</u>. The angel of the Lord appeared to Moses in a flame of fire out of the middle of a bush. He looked and saw that <u>the bush burned with fire, but remarkably, it was not consumed</u>. Moses said, "I will now turn aside and see this great sight why the bush is not burnt." When the Lord saw that he turned aside to see, God called

him out of the middle of the bush by saying, "Moses, Moses!" Moses replied, "Here am I." God said, "Do not come close. Take the shoes off your feet because the place where you stand is holy ground." In addition, God said, "I am the God of your father, the God of Abraham, the God of Isaac, and the God of Jacob." Then, Moses hid his face because he was afraid to look at God. The Lord said, "Surely, I have seen the affliction of My people in Egypt and have heard their cry because of their taskmasters. I know their sorrows. I came down to deliver them from the Egyptians and to bring them out of that land, up to a good and a large land, to a land flowing with milk and honey; to the place of the Canaanites, the Hittites, the Amorites, the Perizzites, the Hivites, and the Jebusites. Indeed, I heard the cry of the children of Israel and I have seen also how the Egyptians oppressed them. Come now *therefore, I will send you to Pharaoh that you may bring My people, the children of Israel out of Egypt." Moses asked God, "Who am I, that I should go to Pharaoh, and that I should bring the children of Israel out of Egypt?" God replied, "Certainly I will be with you. This shall be a **token** that I have sent you; when you bring the people out of Egypt, you shall serve God on **this mountain**." Exodus 3:1-12*

The **token** or sign that God gave Moses as proof that it was God who spoke to him was the fact that Moses would return to Mount Sinai with the people.

The in the meanwhile of faith to this promise was that after Moses brought the Israelites out of bondage in Egypt, God did not allow them to go the direct way to the Promise Land.

It came to pass, when Pharaoh let the people go, God did not lead them through the way of the land of the

*Philistines, although that was near because God said, "Should the people face war, they may want to return to Egypt." But, God led the people a roundabout way, through the way of the wilderness of the Red Sea; and the children of Israel went **ready for war** out of the land of Egypt. Exodus 13:17-18*

The shortest route to the Promised Land would be along the coast of the Mediterranean Sea. **However, the roundabout way that God sent them would make them pass by Mount Sinai.** But, in order to do this they would have to cross the Red Sea. Thus, God performed the miracle of separating the Red Sea so that the Israelites could pass over on dry land (see Exodus 14:21-22). Furthermore, they were not capable of defeating the Egyptians armies that they surely would have encountered along the Mediterranean route. Many Egyptian garrisons heavily protected that route. Soldiers were stationed there to protect what was a major commercial transportation highway.

Then later, on their journey, they witnessed the epiphany of God's presence on Mount Sinai.

The Lord said to Moses, "Go to the people and sanctify them today and tomorrow. Let them wash their clothes and be ready by the third day because on that day the Lord will come down on Mount Sinai in the sight of all the people. You shall set boundaries around the people saying, be careful and do not go up to the mountain, or touch the border of it. Anyone who touches the mountain surely shall be put to death. Should anyone touch it, surely he or she shall be stoned, or shot through, whether a beast or a person, he or she shall not live. When the trumpet makes long sounds, they shall come up to the mountain." Moses went down from the mountain to the *people and sanctified the people. Then they washed their clothes. After that, Moses said to the people, "Be ready by the third day. So, men do not have intimate relations with your wives." <u>And it came to pass on the third day in the morning, that there were thunder and lightning, and a thick cloud on the mountain, and the trumpet made an exceedingly loud noise so that all the people who were in the camp trembled.</u> Then, Moses brought the people out of the camp to meet God. They stood at the foot of the mountain. <u>Mount Sinai was covered entirely with smoke because the Lord descended on it in fire. The smoke ascended like the smoke of a furnace, and the whole mountain shook greatly. When the trumpet sounded long, and became louder and louder, **Moses spoke, and God answered him by a voice**.</u> Then the Lord came down on top of Mount*

Sinai and called Moses up to the top of the mountain. So, Moses went up. After that, the Lord said to Moses, "<u>Go down and warn the people so they will not break through to gaze at the Lord and many of them perish.</u> Let the priests also who come near the Lord sanctify themselves or the Lord will punish them." Exodus 19:10-22

Still, on another occasion, Moses saw on Mount Sinai a demonstration of the awesomeness of God's power.

The Lord said to Moses, "I will do this thing also that you have spoken because you have found grace in My sight, and I know you by your name." Then Moses said, "<u>I beg you, show me Your glory.</u>" The Lord replied, "<u>I will make all My goodness pass before you and I will proclaim the name of the Lord before you.</u> I will be gracious to whom

I will be gracious and will show mercy on whom I will show mercy." In addition, the Lord said, "You cannot see My face because no one can see Me and live." Then the Lord said, "Look, there is a place near Me, there you shall stand on a rock and it shall come to pass, while My glory passes by, that I will put you in a cliff of the rock and will cover you with My hand while I pass by. I will take away My hand and you shall see My back but My face shall not be seen." Exodus 33:17-23

❖ Elijah's Experiences on Mount Carmel

Elijah's name probably means "let God be God." This might be another way of saying, "don't try to control God." Elijah was very disturbed that the Israelites were *limping* trying to serve the god Baal, the goddess Asherah, and the God of Israel at the same time. In I

Kings 18:19, Elijah challenged 450 prophets of Baal and 400 prophets of the goddess Asherah to a showdown on Mount Carmel. Elijah instructed the people to bring two bulls; one for the prophets and the other for him. The bulls were to be prepared for sacrifice then placed on two altars with sticks but without fire. Elijah proposed that the prophets call on their god first, and then he would call on his God. Elijah said that the true God would respond by *fire*. When after all day the many attempts of the prophets failed, Elijah proceeded to call on his God. Fire descended and consumed not only the sacrifice, the sticks, the stones, and the dust, but also the water that was in the trench around the altar. As a result, Elijah ordered the killing of the prophets.

It is recorded in I Kings 19:1-8 that Jezebel, the queen of Israel, vowed to kill the prophet Elijah because he was responsible for the slaying of the prophets of Baal and Asherah. I Kings 19:9-21 tell us that Elijah ran to Mount Horeb (Mount Sinai).

Elijah apparently was not running from Jezebel as much as he was *running to Mount Horeb* to receive from God the same kind of power that Moses experienced on at least the *three* occasions that I mentioned previously in this chapter. After all, Jezebel was not an ordinary threat. She was an extremely zealous high priestess who was the daughter of Ethbaal, the powerful high priest and king of the Zidonians. Customarily, in those days, because Jezebel with her royal and priestly positions came from a dominant society to a lesser one, she had enormous influence in Israel. Essentially, she greatly manipulated King Ahab, her husband. Consequently, Jezebel wielded tremendous power in Israel. She even caused the death of many of Israel's prophets. To the extent that, Elijah felt that he was the only prophet who was serving God. Furthermore, she had personally supported the 400 prophets of the goddess Asherah who Elijah put to death (see I kings, chapters 16-21).

❖ *Elijah's Experience on Mount Horeb (Sinai)*

Elijah said, "I have been very jealous for the almighty God because the children of Israel have forsaken Your covenant, thrown down Your altars, slain Your prophets with the sword; and I am the only prophet left. For that reason they seek my life to take it away." God said, "Go and stand on the **mountain [cliff]** *before the Lord." After awhile the Lord passed by. At that moment, a great and strong wind ripped the mountains and broke the rocks in pieces before the Lord but the Lord was not in the wind. After the wind came an earthquake but the Lord was not in the earthquake. After the earthquake came a fire but the Lord was not in the fire. After the fire came* **a still small voice.** *So, when Elijah heard it, he wrapped his face in his cloak, went* _out, and stood in the entrance of the_ **_cave_**_. After that, a voice said to him, "What are you doing here, Elijah?" Elijah replied, "I have been very jealous for the Almighty God because the children of Israel have forsaken Your covenant, thrown down Your altars, and slain Your prophets with the sword. Only I am left and they seek to take my life." The Lord said to Elijah, "Go return to the wilderness of Damascus. When you get there, anoint Hazael to be king over Syria, anoint Jehu the son of Nimshi king over Israel, and anoint Elisha the son of Shaphat of Abelmeholah prophet in your place." I Kings 19:10-16_

Both Moses and Elijah had extraordinary experiences on Mount Sinai in apparently **the same cave (mountain cliff)** as they witnessed the supernatural presence of the Lord. However, there were some noteworthy differences

between Moses' experiences on Mount Horeb
(Sinai) and those of Elijah.

Moses

- God called out to Moses on Mount
  Sinai to give him power to deliver.
- Moses sought out God on Mount Sinai
  for self-assurance.
- God manifested Himself to Moses with
  impressive occurrences as He gave
  Moses authority to deliver.
- When Moses was depressed, God gave
  him assurances of His presence.

Elijah

- God did not call out to Elijah on Mount
  Sinai. Elijah called on God on Mount
  Carmel.
- Elijah sought out God on Mount Sinai
  for the power of deliverance
- God manifested Himself to Elijah with
  impressive occurrences but answered
  him in a calm way.

- When Elijah was depressed, God questioned his depression and gave him limited authority.

The point of the above story about Elijah is that we shouldn't expect God to act the same way in similar circumstances. God's actions are not always *ordinary*. Sometimes they are *extraordinary*. The extraordinary may not always be spectacular, they can be mundane. God's power is effective either way.

Expect miracles, not just solutions or resolutions. Frequently, we pray expecting that things are going to get better and not for the best that can happen. For example, if your money is limited and you want a vehicle for transportation, don't pray for a bicycle if what you really need is a car. Since nothing is impossible for God, why not ask for miracles. In His own will, He won't always grant us miracles, but ask anyway. Below are two of many scriptures that support the plan that we should develop an attitude of asking God for miracles.

Looking for Miracles

1) **Ephesians 3:20** *Now to Him Who is able to exceed abundantly above all that we ask or think, according to the **power** that works in us.*

2) **John 15:16** *You have not chosen Me but I have chosen you, and ordained you that you should go and bring out fruit, and that your fruit should remain; so that **whatever** you shall ask of the Father in My name, He will give it you.*

We should believe that God is capable of what He promises. By waiting, Abraham and Sarah got a clear message from God that the miracle would not be about them but about Him doing the impossible.

• **Looking for Possibilities**

A good way to expect the impossible is to look for *possibilities*. Scripturally, there are at least three elements of possibilities about things that we regard as impossible.

Principles of Belief and Practices of Faith

1. Believing initiates faith.

Jesus said to him, "If you can believe, all things are <u>possible</u> for the person who believes." Mark 9:23

2. The impossible is also in God's will.

Jesus prayed, "Abba, Father, all things are <u>possible</u> for You; take away this cup from Me, nevertheless, not what I will, but what You will." Mark 14:36

3. With God there are always possibilities.

Jesus looking at them said, "With people it is impossible, but not with God because with God all things are <u>possible</u>." Mark 10:27

• Looking for the Impossible

The biblical statement, "For with God nothing shall be impossible" (Luke 1:37), obviously means that everything is possible for God. For that reason, no believer should ever say, "this or that can't happen." God does not ask us to understand how the impossible become possible. What He asks us to do is to believe. In fact, we should believe that God is about impossibilities simply because *it is impossible for us to understand Him fully.*

• Looking for the Improbable

Matthew 19:26 states that Jesus looked at his disciples and told them, "With people this is impossible but with God all things are possible." The immediate context of this verse shows that at times when God promises what might seem to us to be the impossible; it is simply the *improbable* that He is promising. The context I am referring to is verses twenty-three through thirty of the nineteenth chapter of Matthew. In these verses, Jesus vividly illustrated to the disciples that improbable things could become possible.

Jesus told his disciples that it is difficult for people who depend only on their possessions and not trust in God to enter into the kingdom of heaven. In addition, Jesus said that it is easier to thread a twine made of strands of a camel's hair though the eye of a needle than people who depended on material wealth to enter into the Kingdom of God. When his disciples heard this, they were astonished and wanted to know who could be saved. Jesus made it clear that all things are possible with God. Peter's response was that the disciples had given up a lot to follow Jesus. He questioned what was in it for them. Jesus told the disciples that those who gave up possessions and left families to follow him will eventually become powerful rulers and inherit eternal life. Jesus concluded by stating that many followers who are first will be last and those who are last will be first.

Looking for Miracles

Jesus' illustration appears to be suggesting the impossibility of threading a needle with a cord made of a camel's hair (this is perhaps the best translation and interpretation of the phrase in Aramaic of a "camel going through a needle's eye"). In view of this, there are five things in the dialogue between Jesus and his disciples that suggest that it was the idea of *improbability* that He meant to convey.

First, Jesus compared the many challenges that materialism presents to us as we try to live in ways that are pleasing to God, to threading a needle with many hairs of a camel twisted together.

> *Then Jesus to his disciples, "Truly I tell you, a rich man shall hardly enter into the kingdom of heaven. Again, I say to you, it is easier for a camel to go through the eye of a needle, than for a rich man to enter into the kingdom of God." Matthew 19:23-24*

Second, the disciples understood that Jesus was inferring an improbable situation. Matthew 19:25 indicates that when Jesus' disciples heard it they were very amazed and asked, "Who then can be saved?"

Third, Peter's response indicated that he understood that Jesus was emphasizing an improbability in His illustration. Matthew 19:27 states that Peter said to Jesus, "See, we have left everything and followed you, what then will we have?"

Fourth, Jesus replied that the disciples would have privileged positions in the God's kingdom to come. Jesus declared also that everyone who gave up family and possessions for His sake will receive more than what they lost. Additionally, the fact that those who will receive new blessings will not lose them was underscored when Jesus said in Matthew 19:29 that those who made sacrifices to follow Him will "keep those things forever."

Fifth, Jesus summarized the entire message on improbabilities by saying in Matthew 19:30,

"But many who are first shall be <u>last; and the last</u> shall be first." Notice that the double chiasm emphasizes **"last"** (chiasm is a term used in biblical studies reflecting a particular genre of writing and teaching where the main point comes in the center). The last being first is not necessarily impossible, just improbable.

• Believing in the Impossible

If all things are possible with God then His promises must include the impossible. In that case, God often promises the impossible. *I must reiterate here that this is not a matter of understanding. It is a matter of believing. We cannot understand the impossible anyway.*

When I think about God doing the impossible, I frequently remember a story that my grandmother told me many times. My grandmother gave birth to several children but they all died soon after birth. Several doctors told my grandmother that it would be impossible for her to have a child that would survive for a long time after birth. Eventually, she gave birth to a son who survived infancy only to die by a tragic accident when he was a toddler. He choked on a piece of meat given to him by a neighbor. Finally, my grandmother gave birth to a baby girl who would become my mother. The doctors gave my grandmother little hope for the survival of the baby who was born extremely ill. My grandmother, believing the impossible, prayed to God for a miracle. God answered her in a vision. God told her to take the child to a church of a denomination with which she had issues. Nevertheless, my grandmother obeyed God. The child was dedicated in the church to God. My mother lived for nearly eighty years! My grandmother never had another child.

Believing the impossible is a joke. When God told Abraham that he would have a son with Sarah he thought that it was a joke. *Abraham laughed!*

> *God said to Abraham, "As for Sarai your wife, you shall not call her name Sarai, but Sarah shall be her name. I*

will bless her and give you a son of her. Indeed, I will bless her and she shall be a mother of nations; kings of people shall come from her." Then Abraham fell with his face level to the ground and <u>*laughed*</u>*. He said in his heart, "Shall a child be born to him that is a hundred years old? Shall Sarah, who is ninety years old, bear a child?" At that moment, Abraham said to God, "If only Ishmael might be the blessings that God wants!" God answered, "Sarah your wife shall bear you a son, indeed, and you shall call his name Isaac; and I will establish an everlasting covenant with him, and with his generations after him." Genesis 17:15-19*

On a later occasion, Sarah overheard three men speaking to Abraham apparently on behalf of God. They said that she would have a son with her husband. *Sarah thought that it was a joke and laughed within herself!*

The men said to Abraham, "Where is Sarah your wife?" He answered, "Look in the tent." Then one of the men said, "I will certainly return to you at a given time and Sarah shall have a son." Sarah heard this through the tent door that was behind Abraham. Now, Abraham and Sarah were old and well advanced in age. Sarah's age was beyond childbearing. Accordingly, Sarah laughed within herself saying, "After I am old shall I have pleasure; my husband being old also?" The Lord said to Abraham, "Why did Sarah laugh, saying, 'Shall I surely bear a child when I am old?' Is anything too hard for the Lord? At the appointed time, I will return and Sarah shall have a son." Then Sarah denied what she said by saying, "I did not laugh." She said this because she was afraid. Therefore, the Lord stated, "Certainly, you did laugh." Genesis 18: 9-15

Abraham and Sarah had a son who, not surprisingly, God gave the name Isaac (see Genesis 17:19). Isaac means "one who laughs." *Therefore, God always has the last laugh!*

• **Expect More Than We Seek**

These all died in faith not having received the promises but having seen them from far, and were persuaded of them… Hebrews 11:13

In a sense, the Principles of Belief that we follow can affect the faith of others after we die. The expression "these all died in faith" in the above verse means that they believed God's promises. Consequently, they died expecting actions of faith on our part. Likewise, while we are living, we may not receive all the blessings that we expect but we can die believing that those blessings will continue with others who have the faith *to act on our beliefs.*

Therefore, an element of this Principle of Belief is to *expect more than we seek.* Expect more than miracles and even more than things *we think are impossible!* In other words, don't be surprised by anything that God does. Abraham and Sarah were rich when they prayed to be blessed with a son. They wanted a way to pass on their blessings, even though; a promise by God was given to them already through Ishmael.

> *As for Ishmael, I have heard you. Watch, I have blessed him, and will make him have many children. I will multiply his generations abundantly. Twelve princes will come through him. I will make him a great nation. Genesis 17:20*

Nevertheless, Abraham and Sarah wanted to go beyond the promise through Ishmael. They wanted a promise of their very own; a promise through a son procreated by both of them.

Some of my most significant blessings came because I didn't settle for just the blessings that God gave me when I believed and expected that He had more for me. A case in point, God blessed me to become a teacher. But, I wanted to do more with my teaching skills. So, God called me to be a minister. Now, I teach God's Word. In other words, *I was blessed to be a teacher but now as a minister of God, I teach to be blessed.*

We should expect more than we seek because:

- ❏ Why jump when we can leap?
- ❏ Why leap when we can fly?
- ❏ Why fly when we can soar?

• **Seek More Than We Expect**

If we expect more than we seek then there are times we should *seek more than we expect.* Parts of the prayer in Ephesians 3:14-19 exemplify the seeking qualities of detecting, prospecting, and projecting.

For this cause, I bow my knees to the Father of our Lord Jesus Christ, of Whom the whole family in heaven and earth is named. I pray that God may <u>grant you according to the riches of His glory, mighty strength by His Spirit in you.</u> May Christ dwell in your hearts by faith, that you, being rooted and grounded in love, <u>may be able to comprehend with all the saints what is the breadth, length, depth, and height of that love. Christ's love surpasses our knowledge. I also pray that you may be filled with all the fullness of God. Now, to Him who is able to exceed abundantly above all that we ask or think, according to the power that works in us,</u> be glory in the church by Christ Jesus throughout all ages, world without end. Amen.

Detecting

We are rich according to God's glory. This is emphasized from the beginning of the book of Ephesians. Essentially, Ephesians 1:18 is pivotal to this understanding of our relationship with Christ:

> *I pray that the eyes of your understanding may be enlightened. I pray also that you may know what the hope of His calling is, and what are the <u>riches of the glory of His inheritance in the saints.</u>*

Many Christians are not good spiritual detectives. For instance, they fail to discover that Christ grants us many blessings that come from His strength within us. Since they are grants, they require nothing on our part except to seek them. That's our faith.

Prospecting

We have great prospects for blessings because God gives us connections with other saints. To "comprehend" with the saints is to network in a "prehensile" manner. The word comprehend is connected to the root meaning of prehensile. It is to "grasp quickly," especially by wrapping around something. If we are seeking, for instance, job opportunities, we should quickly network with other saints. This is one of many important reasons for becoming a member of a church. Furthermore, we are uniquely fashioned and placed in the Body of Christ. This is indicated in Ephesians 2:10:

> *We are his workmanship. We are created in Christ Jesus to good works that God prepared for us in advance as our way of living.*

The word workmanship is translated from the Greek word, *poiema*. We get the word poem from *poiema*. Therefore, we are purposely prepared by God to be who we are! *We are God's masterpieces!*

Projecting
Our projection must be inclusive and extensive enough that we think universally and not

locally or even globally. The book of Ephesians highlights Jesus as a Christ of the universe, indeed, of all existence. We see this fact from the beginning of the book.

> *God placed Christ far above all governments, powers, authorities, kingdoms, and every name that is named, not only in this world, but also in that which is to come. God has put all things under Jesus' feet, and made Him the Head over all things in the church, which is His body, the fullness of Him that fills all in all. Ephesians 1:21-23*

That's why; verse thirteen of the fourth chapter is probably the key point of the book:

> *Until we all come in the unity of the faith, and of the knowledge of the Son of God, to a maturity that becomes the <u>full measure of the stature of the fullness of Christ.</u>*

I call this concept of maturing in Christ the "big bang" result of being "rooted and grounded" in Him to the extent that we realize the real magnitude of the "breadth, length, depth, and height" of His love. In other words, we are always spiritually expanding and contracting at the same time from Christ in us to the centrality of His entire existence.

Therefore, the benediction in Paul's prayer in Ephesians 3:20-21 gives us a **context** to seek more than we expect.

> *Now, to Him who is able to exceed abundantly <u>above all that we ask or think</u>, according to the power that works in us, to Him be glory in the church by Christ Jesus throughout all ages, world without end. Amen.*

Hence, when we seek miracles expect them to be:

- ○ deeper than we can **detect**
- ○ larger than our **prospect**

Looking for Miracles

- ○ longer than our **project**
- ○ wider than our **context**

God blessed both Isaac and Ishmael as progenitors of great nations according to His promises.

> *God said to Abraham, "Indeed, Sarah your wife shall bear you a son and you shall call his name Isaac. I will establish My covenant with him for an everlasting covenant, and with his descendants. As for Ishmael, I have heard you. Watch, I have blessed him, and will make him have many children, and will multiply his generations abundantly. Twelve princes will come through him. I will make him a great nation. Nevertheless, My covenant I will establish with Isaac, who Sarah shall bear for you at this set time next year. Genesis 17:19-21*

We should not be astonished by the answers to our prayers. They can be more than we imagine. In the case of Abraham and Sarah, God gave them two blessed sons. These blessings are extended to many people even to this day.

From time to time, many health professionals become burnt-out because of the nature of their practices. Dr. Frances Brisbane, the Dean of the School of Social Welfare of the State University of New York at Stony Brook, sometimes refers to these experiences as "compassion fatigue." I imagine that frequently contributing to the compassion fatigue of those who regularly assist others with personal issues, is a feeling of discouragement because their own lives may not be going well. For instance, many Christians regularly help needy people. Nevertheless, their own lives are chaotic. In spite of their good works, they may be affected by personal and family crises, financial challenges, and health difficulties. *However, they should keep seeking more blessings than they expect even though good things might seem elusive for them.* They should be encouraged by the fact that all things are possible with God. Abraham and Sarah did not have the slightest clue that they would bring into this world the Messiah who would save all of us. For Abraham and for us it is more than we can see, more than we can imagine, and more than what we dream. Finally, not only is **anything that is "more than" possible with God but even "more than" the impossible is possible with Him!**

• God Is About the Living Not the Dead

When we emulate the people of faith in eleventh chapter of Hebrews, we should not think of them as "dead people." Overall, we should think of things related to belief and faith as being alive. For this reason, those people of faith are "alive to us."

For many religious people in Jesus' time, Abraham, the other patriarchs, and the prophets (they would include some of the people of faith) were simply dead. The legacies of belief and faith of their ancestors were not necessarily dynamic and meaningful to many people in the time of Jesus. On the contrary, Jesus stipulated that Abraham's faith was very much alive to Him. Furthermore, Jesus claimed that He existed before Abraham. Jesus also said that because He existed before Abraham, the patriarch's faith was connected to God.

> *Then said the Jews to Jesus, "Now we know that You have a demon. Abraham died, and the prophet died, and You say, 'People who follow My teachings will never die.' Are You greater than our father Abraham, who is dead? Also, the prophets are dead, so who are You?" Jesus answered, "If I honor Myself, My honor is nothing. My Father honors Me. You say that He is your God, yet, you have not known Him, but I know Him. If I should say, I do not know Him; I would be a liar like you. However, I know Him and follow His word. Your father Abraham rejoiced to see My day. He saw it and was glad."*

Looking for Miracles

Then the Jews asked him, "You are not yet fifty years old and You have seen Abraham?" Jesus responded, "Honestly, I tell you, before Abraham was, I am." Then they took up stones to cast at Him but Jesus hid Himself, and then went out of the temple, going through the midst of them, and so passed by. John 8:52-59

On another occasion, Jesus indicated that Moses recognized the living presence of the patriarchs' faith as he witnessed the epiphany of a bush burning and not being consumed by fire.

Even Moses clearly demonstrated at the bush that the dead are raised to life when he addressed the Lord as the God of Abraham, Isaac, and Jacob. Now, He is not the God of the dead, but of the living because to Him all of them are alive. Luke 20:37-38

Perhaps, the most dramatic and direct account that indicates that God is about the living, resulted from a confrontation between the Sadducees and Jesus. The Sadducees did not believe in the resurrection of the dead. So, they questioned Jesus about the resurrection of the dead. They used a hypothetical scenario of a woman marrying seven brothers. The marriages took place after the death of each brother. Lastly, the woman died. The Sadducees wanted to know from Jesus whose wife she would be in the resurrection (see Mark 12: 18 -23). Here is Jesus' reply.

> *Jesus answering told them, "You are incorrect because you do not know the Scriptures, neither the power of God. When the dead rise, they will not marry. They will be like angels who are in heaven." Mark 12:24-25*

The point is that the resurrection of the dead is about "living," while what we know as "life" is ultimately about "dying." We cannot equate the two because living is beyond the experience of dying!

One of the themes of the Sabbatical Laws or Forgiveness Laws found in Leviticus 25:1-15 is that God is about the living (see Principles of Belief and Practices of Faith One, Giving and Receiving is Forgiving). For example, one of the laws states that planting and reaping were to done for six years then in the seventh (sabbatical) year the land was to be given rest. God would provide enough food in the planting years to last the entire sabbatical year.

Actually, the custom of leaving a section of land fallow is not about the death of the land, it's about giving life to it. When a portion of land is ploughed and left unseeded for at least a planting season, the soil recovers its natural fertility. In many parts of the world where portions of lands are not left unplanted for a period, it is reasonable to attribute floods and famine from the resulting conditions. Too much cultivation of a section of land without crop-free stages can cause the erosion of the soil thus resulting in floods. Additionally, the depletion of the soil's natural chemicals by too much planting without resting the soil can lead to poor crops and therefore inadequate amount of food supply.

• **Jubilee**

After seven sabbatical years, there was a *jubilee* year. In this year of celebration, all properties were returned to their original owners or their descendants

Jesus proclaimed that we are in the time of jubilee until His second coming. This is clear in comparing the following two passages of scriptures.

The first passage is an Old Testament prophecy.

> *The Spirit of the Lord God is on Me because the Lord has anointed Me to preach good news to the meek. He sent Me to heal the brokenhearted, to proclaim liberty to the captives, to open the prison for them who are bound,*

to proclaim the acceptable year of the Lord; and the day of vengeance of our God, to comfort all who mourn, to provide for them who mourn in Zion, to give them beauty for ashes, the oil of joy for mourning, the garment of praise for the spirit of heaviness; that they might be called trees of righteousness, the planting of the Lord that He might be glorified. Isaiah 61:1-3

The second passage is the fulfillment of part of the prophecy.

Jesus returned in the power of the Spirit to Galilee and his fame spread throughout the region. He taught in their synagogues and was glorified by everyone. Then, He came to Nazareth where He had been brought up and as His custom was, He went into the synagogue on the Sabbath day, and stood to read. The book of the prophet Esaias was delivered to Him.

When He opened the book, He found the place where it was written, "The Spirit of the Lord is on Me because He has anointed Me to preach the gospel to the poor. He has sent Me to heal the brokenhearted, to preach deliverance to the captives, to recover the sight of the blind, to give liberty to those who are oppressed, and to preach the acceptable year of the Lord." He closed the book, gave it again to the minister, and sat down. The eyes of all the people in the synagogue were fixed on Him. Luke 4:14-20

Jesus quoted Isaiah 61:1-2 to describe His ministry. He did this at the start of His ministry. Since Jesus was giving a description of His ministry, we can interpret this to mean that He was referring only to His "first coming."

Therefore, when Jesus read Isaiah 61:1-2, He virtually stopped in the middle of a sentence (for us, this is the middle of verse 2). Jesus deliberately stopped short because the rest of the sentence would describe His "second com-ing" (this is verse 3 for us).

Jesus' first coming was about His life and ministry as described in the four gospels of the Bible. An account in Mark 6:17-19 related to John the Baptizer's imprisonment by King Herod Antipas explains Jesus' first coming. When John the Baptizer was in prison, he sent two of his disciples to Jesus to inquire whether He was really the Messiah. This is how Jesus re-sponded.

> *Then Jesus answering said to them, "Go and tell John what things you have seen and heard; how the blind see, the lame walk, the lepers are cleansed, the deaf hear, the dead are raised, and to the poor the gospel is preached." Luke 7:22*

Jesus' reply definitely underscored the fact that He fulfilled the description of the ministry of His first coming as stated in Isaiah 61:1-2.

Principles of Belief and Practices of Faith

Jesus' second coming refers to a time in the future when He will return as an avenger of evil and a judge of the unrighteous. For example, Jesus second coming is described in Revelation 1:7.

> *Look, He will come on clouds. Every eye shall see Him, and they also who pierced Him. All nations of the earth shall weep in sorrow because of Him. It will be so. Amen.*

Here are other ways to understand the differences between Jesus' first and second comings.

In Jesus' first coming He was the **lamb** without a spot or blemish who was sacrificed for the sins of the world (see John 1:36 and I Peter 1:19). Also, in Jesus' first coming, He was "led as a sheep to the slaughter; and like a dumb **lamb** before his shearer, so He opened not His mouth" (Acts 8:32).

In contrast, at Jesus' second coming the evil people will say to the mountains and rocks,

"Fall on us, and hide us from the face of Him who sits on the throne, and from the wrath of the **Lamb** because the great day of his wrath is come; and who shall be able to stand?" (Revelation 6:16-17).

Indeed, Jesus stopped at the phrase "the acceptable year of the Lord." *The acceptable year of the Lord is the jubilee year.* Incidentally, the jubilee year started on the Day of Atonement. This is the day when God forgave the sins of the people through the rituals of the High Priest.

Sin is equated to death. Romans 6:23 says, "For the wages of sin is death; but the gift of God is eternal life through Jesus Christ our Lord." *Atonement is equated to life.* Romans 5:11 says, "We also joy in God through our Lord Jesus Christ, by Whom we have now received the atonement" (reconciliation). *Therefore, because of Jesus' sacrificial death we are living in the acceptable (Jubilee) year of the Lord!*

PRINCIPLE AND PRACTICE SIX
Attaching no Strings

By faith Abraham, when he was tried, offered Isaac as a sacrifice to God. He who received the promises offered as sacrifice his only begotten son. Of whom it was said, "Your descendant shall come through Isaac." Abraham believed that God could raise the dead. Therefore, as a figure (type), God raised Isaac from the dead. Hebrews 11:17-19

Acting in faith with no strings attached is to believe in God without conditions of blessings. We often pray with conditions. Sometimes, we call this, "bargaining with God." For example, when we say, "God, if you will help me out of this mess, I will do this or that for you," this is bargaining with God.

Bargaining with God in itself is not a bad thing, necessarily. Abraham bargained with

God when he was maturing in faith. Soon after God's messengers promised Abraham and Sarah a son in their old age (see the Believing in the Impossible section in the previous chapter of this book and Genesis 18:9-15) the Bible records an incident of bargaining between Abraham and God.

> *The men rose up and looked toward Sodom. Abraham went to send them on their way. Then the Lord said, "Shall I hide from Abraham the thing that I do, seeing that Abraham shall surely become a great and mighty nation and all the nations of the earth shall be blessed in him? For I know him, he will command his children and his household. They will keep the way of the Lord, doing what is just and right, so that the Lord may bring on Abraham that which He has spoken of him." In addition, the Lord said, "The cry of Sodom and Gomorrah is great, and their sin is very serious, I will go*

down and see whether or not what I heard is correct." The men went toward Sodom but Abraham remained with the Lord. Abraham approached the Lord and asked, "Will You also destroy the righteous with the wicked? Suppose there are fifty righteous people within the city, will You also destroy the place and not spare the innocent people who are there? Far be it from You to slay the righteous with the wicked. Shall not the Judge of all the earth do right?" The Lord replied, "If I find in Sodom fifty righteous people, then I will spare the entire place for their sakes." Abraham said, "See now, I have taken it upon myself to speak to the Lord. I am but dust and ashes. Suppose there are forty-five righteous people, will You still destroy the entire city?" The Lord replied, "If I find there forty-five righteous people, I will not destroy it." Abraham spoke to the Lord yet again and said, "Suppose forty

*righteous people are found there?"
The Lord replied, "I will not do it for the
sake of forty righteous people." Then
Abraham said to Lord, "Oh, let not the
Lord be angry, and I will speak. Suppose thirty righteous people are found
there?" The Lord replied "I will not do
it if I find thirty there." Abraham said,
"See now, I have taken it upon me to
speak to the Lord. What if there are
twenty righteous people there?" The
Lord replied, "I will not destroy it for
the sake of twenty righteous people."
Abraham said again, "Oh, let not the
Lord be angry, and I will speak yet
but this last time; what if ten righteous people are found there?" The
Lord replied, "I will not destroy it for
ten righteous people's sake." The Lord
went His way as soon as He stopped
speaking with Abraham. Then, Abraham returned to his place. Genesis
18:16-33*

Attaching no Strings

Of course, Genesis 19:24-25 recorded that God destroyed the cities of Sodom and Gomorrah.

Nevertheless, there are instances in the Bible where bargaining with God culminated in good results. For instance, 2 Kings 20:11 records that King Hezekiah was very sick and was about to die. In fact, God told him so. After praying to God, Hezekiah's life was extended fifteen more years. It is clear that Hezekiah bargained with God for more time to live. Hezekiah's bargaining was based on the good things he did in the past and what he wanted to do in the future. Still, two acts of faith accompanied the miracle. First, the prophet Isaiah applied medication to a boil on Hezekiah. Second, Hezekiah asked for a sign that he would recover and God made the shadow on a sundial go backward ten steps as the king requested to see as proof.

Often, bargaining with God involves little faith on our part, as in the case of Abraham and Sodom and Gomorrah. Therefore, sometimes bargaining with God is limited to our wishes. It often does not in essence engage the faith to change a situation. Then, even when bargaining with God is successful, it might still require acts of faith, as in the case of Hezekiah. Therefore, bargaining with God is definitely not as effective as unconditional trust in Him.

Furthermore, faith relates to believing in God's promises while at times bargaining is negotiating outside the covenant that God has with us. God's covenant with us centers on promises that He made with Abraham.

When Abraham attempted to sacrifice Isaac, we see that the fundamentals of the "Principle of Belief and the Practice of Faith of Attaching no Strings" are more successful than bargaining with God.

> *By faith Abraham, when he was tried, offered Isaac as a sacrifice to God. Hebrews 11:17*

Hebrews 11:17 is referring to Genesis 22:1-18. This passage of Scripture tells how God "tested"

Abraham. God asked Abraham to sacrifice his son Isaac as a burnt offering to the Lord. Abraham trusted God and did not bargain with Him.

The story is a culmination of Abraham's faith walk. It is clear that there are gradual developments in the process of Abraham *walking by faith for God.* Abraham literally walked about as a nomad as he grew in faith. He followed God in the elements of belief and faith as described by Jesus in Luke 9:57-62 where He illustrated who are true followers of His way. This I call *followship* and it is elaborated in the fourth Principle of Belief and Practice of Faith. Accordingly, I term Abraham's faith walk *followship.*

Underscoring the element of followship at this juncture of Abraham's faith walk are many typologies, symbolic meanings, and imageries relating to Jesus.

- o **Isaac was the "only begotten Son" of Abraham and Jesus was the only begotten son of God.** (This typing is referred to in the Faith and Typology section on p. 25)

He who received the promises offered as sacrifice His only begotten Son. Hebrews 11:17

o **Isaac was supposed to be a substitute lamb for a sacrificial burnt offering whereas Jesus was crucified as the Sacrificial Lamb of God** (this typing is referred to in the Faith and Typology section on p. 25).

God said, "Take your only son, Isaac … to Moriah and offer him as a burnt offering on one of the mountains." Genesis 22:2

o **Isaac was to be sacrificed on a specific mountain. Jesus was crucified on Golgotha. Many people believe that Golgotha was a specific part of a hill.**

Attaching no Strings

God said to Abraham, "I will tell you which mountain." Genesis 22:2

○ **Abraham laid on Isaac's back the wood to be burned when he would become a sacrificial offering. Jesus was made to carry on His back the wooden cross on which He was killed** (this typing is referred to in the Faith and Typology section on p. 25).

Abraham took the wood of the burnt offering and laid it on Isaac his son... Genesis 22:6

○ **Because of the fire, Isaac was going to be a complete sacrifice. Jesus was a complete sacrifice for us.**

Abraham also took the fire in his hand... Genesis 22:6

○ **The knife that would have been used to stab Isaac reminds us that Jesus was**

pierced in His side with a spear after He died on the cross.

Abraham took a knife… Genesis 22:6

o **In the symbolism below, two young men accompanied Abraham and Isaac. Although the two men did not go to the place of sacrifice, it reminds us that Jesus was sacrificed on the cross with two men.**

Abraham rose up early in the morning and saddled his donkey. Abraham took with him two of his young men and his son Isaac. Abraham cut the wood for the burnt offering and went to the place about which God told him. Genesis 22:3

• The Third Day

Generic to the types mentioned above is the symbolism of the "third day." Genesis 22:4

states, "Then on the third day Abraham lifted up his eyes, and saw the place far away." In the story of Abraham's attempt to sacrifice Isaac, we discover something significant about Abraham seeing the place of sacrifice from a distance on the third day. Considering God's instructions to Abraham to sacrifice Isaac, even without knowing the end of the story, we could assume that God would deliver Isaac because of the third day. This symbolism strongly suggests that Isaac would not be sacrificed on the third day because of at least two specific types.

1. God spared the lives of the people on Mount Sinai because they were prepared for Him on the third day.

Before God gave the Law to the people on Mount Sinai (Mount Horeb), He gave Moses instructions for them:

"Go to the people and sanctify them to-day and tomorrow. Let them wash their clothes and be ready by the third day

because on that third day the Lord will come down on Mount Sinai in the sight of all the people." Exodus 19:10-11

People cannot see God and live (see Exodus 33:20). God came down from Mount Sinai on the third day. The people's lives were spared because they did not cross a boundary to see Him (see Exodus 19:16-23).

2. Jesus rose from the dead on the third day.

Now when evening came, because it was the day before the Sabbath, Joseph of Arimathaea, a respected member of the council, who also waited for the kingdom of God, went boldly to Pilate and petitioned the body of Jesus. Pilate marveled that Jesus was already dead. Pilate called the centurion and asked him if Jesus had been dead for a while. When the centurion told Pilate that Jesus was dead, he gave *the body to Joseph. Joseph bought fine linen, took Jesus down, wrapped Him in the linen, laid Him in a sepulcher that was hewn out of a rock, and rolled a stone in front of the door of the sepulcher. Mary Magdalene and Mary the mother of Joses saw where Jesus was laid. When the <u>Sabbath was past</u>, Mary Magdalene, Mary the mother of James, and Salome, bought sweet spices that they might come and anoint him. Very early in the morning of the <u>first day of the week,</u> they came to the sepulcher at the rising of the sun. They asked among themselves, "Who shall roll away the stone from the door of the sepulcher for us?" When they looked, they saw that the very large stone was rolled away. They entered the sepulcher and saw a young man sitting on the right side, clothed in a long white garment; and they were afraid. He said to them, "Be not afraid. You seek Jesus of Nazareth, Who was* *crucified. He is risen. He is not here. Look, this is the place where they laid Him. Mark 15:42-16:6*

• **Confidence in God**

The linguistic source of the English word *confidence* literally means "with faith." Abraham had already developed great confidence in God over the years when God called him to sacrifice Isaac. The passage of scripture below gives us an idea of the extent that Abraham had grown in his *walk by faith for God* (see Principles of Belief and Practices of Faith, Four).

❖ **Abraham was confident that he and Isaac would return after the sacrifice.**

*Abraham said to his young men, "Stay here with the donkey. **The lad and I will… return to you**." Genesis 22:5*

238

• **Affirmation in God**

God instructed Abraham to sacrifice his beloved son Isaac because there is something beyond confidence in terms of faith. I call it "affirmation." Etymologically affirmation is related to the verb "to strengthen." Therefore, when I use the word affirmation in terms of belief and faith I mean the strengthening of our confidence in God.

God told Abraham to sacrifice the very son that He promised him. In this instance, God required more than confidence from Abraham. Abraham had grown tremendously in faith. Still, God wanted Abraham, in spite of his blessings, to have faith in Him. In the attempted sacrifice of Isaac, we can type Abraham's moving from confidence to affirmation in God to that of Jesus' moving from confidence to affirmation in God. This is regarding Jesus' death on the cross. The following particulars are the comparisons:

❖ **Abraham was confident that God would not "break The Promise."**

Abraham said to his young men, "Stay here with the donkey. The lad and I will go over there and worship…" Genesis 22:5

❖ **Abraham affirmed that "God Himself" would provide an alternative sacrifice**

Isaac spoke to Abraham, his father, and said, "My father!" Abraham replied, "Here am I, my son." Then Isaac said, "I see that we have the things to start the fire and the wood, but where is the lamb for a burnt offering?" Abraham answered, "My son, God will provide Himself a lamb for a burnt of-

fering." So, both of them went together.
Genesis 22:7-8

❖ Jesus was confident that for Him God's "will" would be best.

When Jesus came out of the agony of anticipating His sacrificial death on the cross, He ended His prayer this way:

> *Jesus said, "Abba, Father, all things are possible for you; take away this cup from Me. Nevertheless, not what I will, but what You will." Mark 14:36*

❖ Jesus affirmed that God would "secure" a spiritual life for Him.

Dr. Frances Brisbane has a gift of matching people and their circumstances to motivational and inspirational maxims on cards and page markers that she gives them. When I was thinking about this segment of this chapter, Dr. Brisbane gave me a page marker relating to the last thing that Jesus said on the cross to His Father. It made me realize that perhaps what Jesus said reflected the best example of someone moving from confidence in God to affirmation in God.

The last statement that Jesus made before His sacrificial death on the cross is below:

> Jesus shouted with a loud voice, "Father, into Your hands I give My spirit!" Having said this, He gave up His life. Luke 23:46

Like Abraham, Jesus, and other people of faith, while we are growing in faith, our confidence builds to affirmation. This is important because *God wants us to love Him for **Himself** and not for the blessings that He gives us, or for the difficulties that we might experience for His sake.*

• **A Ram and Not a Lamb**

In the Bible, the word Lamb generally means a young sheep. However, in Exodus 12:3-6, the word lamb referred to either a young sheep or *a young goat*. At times, the word lamb may have included also an adult animal (for instance, see Leviticus 4:35).

There are many implications typing Jesus as the Sacrificial Lamb of God. As I previously mentioned, in John 1:29 Jesus is called the Sacrificial Lamb of God. Also, there are messianic prophecies that suggest that Jesus would be the Sacrificial Lamb of God. For instance,

> *He was oppressed and afflicted, yet He did not open His mouth. He was brought as a lamb to the slaughter. As a sheep before her shearers is silent, so He did not open His mouth. Isaiah 53:7*

It is fair to assume that Abraham fully expected God to provide a lamb as a young sheep or a young goat and most likely a male. This would be in keeping with the long established sacrificial system and the Passover (for examples, see Genesis 4:4 and Exodus 12:5). *But, God provided a grown male sheep.*

Abraham and Isaac came to the place where God had told Abraham to go. Abraham built an altar there, laid the wood in order, bound Isaac, his son, and laid him on the wood of the altar. Then, Abraham stretched forward his hand and took the knife to slay his son. At that moment, the angel of the Lord spoke to him from heaven and said, "Abraham, Abraham!" Abraham answered, "Here am I." A voice said, "Do not lay your hand on the lad, or hurt him in any way because now I know that you are obedient to God, seeing that you have not withheld your son, your only son from me." Abraham lifted up his eyes and looked. He saw behind him that there was a <u>ram caught in a</u>

bush by his horns. Therefore, Abraham went and took the ram and offered him as a burnt offering instead of his son. So, Abraham called the name of that place Jehovah-jireh, as it is said to this day, on the Lord's mountain, He shall provide. Genesis 22:9-14

Now, sheep are closely related to goats. This is very evident in the male sheep. The grown male sheep, of course, can easily be typed to Jesus. Yet, there is something else. Is there a type here between the scapegoat and Jesus? The scapegoat was part of the sacrificial ritual of the Day of Atonement. I will explain this later.

If we expect more from God, then we should never take what He does for granted. Neither, can we expect God to act the same way all the time. In other words, how God acted in the past does not obligate him to act similarly in the future. Furthermore, there are several places in the Bible where we find instances of God clearly giving us the message that we should not take Him or His promises for granted.

Actually, we should not take anything about God for granted. However, because God is all-powerful, one area in which we frequently take God for granted is in His power to change situations. *Often, we seek more power from God after we take for granted the power that He first gives us.*

As I previously mentioned, Elijah ran to Mount Sinai to get power similar to that of Moses so that he could deal with a death threat from Jezebel. However, Moses himself sought more power from God to deal with the difficult challenges that he kept experiencing in leading the people of Israel. Below are three experiences of Moses with God that show how we often take it for granted that God should always give us power.

1) **God Called Moses to Power**

In Exodus chapter 3, Moses received power from God to do ministry.

> *Moses said to God, "Look, when I go to the children of Israel and say to*

them, the God of your fathers sent me to you, if they say to me, 'What is his name?' what should I say to them?" God told Moses, "I AM THAT I AM." Additionally God said, "Thus you shall say to the children of Israel, I AM has sent me to you." Moreover, God said to Moses, "Thus you shall say to the children of Israel, the Lord God of your fathers, the God of Abraham, the God of Isaac, and the God of Jacob, has sent me to you. This is My name forever. This is My name for all generations." Exodus 3:13-15

When God calls us to do His will, we are automatically given power in His name to undertake the mission or the ministry.

2) **Moses Called God for Power**

In Exodus chapter 33, Moses pleaded with God for more power to do ministry

Moses said to the Lord, "See, You tell me, 'Bring up this people' and You have not told me who You will send with me. You said, 'I know you by name and I have favored you.' Now therefore, I appeal to You, if I am favored by You, show me again Your power that I may know You, that I may know that I am favored by You. Remember that this nation is Your people." God replied, "My presence will go with you, and I will give you <u>success</u>." Then Moses said to God, "If You do not go with me, do not let me leave here." Exodus 33:12-15

3) <u>God Confirmed Moses' Power</u>

However, God had given Moses already all the power that he needed including the means and authority to use it. This is clear in the passage of Scripture below.

Moses answered, "But, look, they will not believe me, or even listen to me *because they will say, 'The Lord did not appear to you.'" The Lord asked Moses, <u>"What is that in your hand?" He answered, "A rod!"</u> Then God said, "Throw it to the ground." Moses threw the rod to the ground and it became a snake. Then Moses fled from it. The Lord said to Moses, "Stretch out your hand and take it by the tail." Moses extended his hand and picked up the snake. The snake became a rod in his hand. God told Moses, <u>"This is how they will believe that the Lord God of their fathers, the God of Abraham, the God of Isaac, and the God of Jacob, has appeared to you.</u>" Exodus 4:1-5*

• **The Promise Fulfilled**

As we have seen several times before, God promised Abraham that his descendants would be blessed. Still, God asked Abraham to sacrifice his "only begotten son." When God made this request of Abraham, God had fulfilled His part of the promise already. God was waiting only for Abraham to fulfill his part of the promise. This is evident in the scriptural passage below.

> *The angel of the Lord called Abraham from heaven the second time and said, "<u>I have sworn by Myself because you have done this thing and have not withheld your son, your only son, certainly, I will bless you.</u> I will multiply your descendants as the stars of the sky and as the sand on the seashore. Your descendants shall possess the gate of their enemies. From your descendants shall all the nations of the earth be blessed because you have obeyed my voice." Genesis 22:15-18*

Often, when God makes promises to us, He waits for us to be obedient by fulfilling our part of the promise. Overall, we fulfill our part of the promise through our belief and faith in God.

• Scapegoat

Lots were cast for two goats on the Day of Atonement.

> *Aaron shall take the two goats and present them before the Lord at the door of the tent of the congregation. Aaron shall cast lots on the two goats, one lot for the Lord's goat and the other lot for the scapegoat. Leviticus 16:7-8*

The first goat was sacrificed as a sin offering.

> *Aaron shall bring the goat on which the Lord's lot fell and offer him as a sin offering. Leviticus 16:8*

The second goat was the "scapegoat."

However, the goat on which the lot fell to be the scapegoat shall be presented alive before the Lord for atonement and be let go into the wilderness. Leviticus 16: 10

We can connect the goat for the sin offering to the sacrificial lamb.

Then Aaron shall kill the goat of the sin offering for the people and bring his blood inside the curtain to do with it as he did with the blood of the bullock. Aaron shall sprinkle the blood on the mercy seat. Before the mercy seat, Aaron shall make atonement for the holy place because of the uncleanness of the children of Israel and for their transgressions and all their sins. Aaron shall make atonement for the tent of the congregation that is with them in the midst of their uncleanness.

Attaching no Strings

There shall be no person in the tent of the congregation when Aaron goes in to make atonement in the holy place until he comes out and have made atonement for himself, for his household, and for all the congregation of Israel. Leviticus 16: 15-17

We can connect the scapegoat to the sacrificial lamb.

When Aaron finishes reconciling the holy place, the tent of the congregation, and the altar, he shall bring in the live goat. Aaron shall put both of his hands on the head of the live goat. Aaron shall confess over the goat all the iniquities of the children of Israel and all the transgressions of all their sins. He shall transfer them on the head of the goat. A man appointed to the task shall carry the goat into the wilderness. The man shall send the goat carrying all the iniquities of the people into the wilderness to an uninhabited land. Aaron shall come into the tent of the congregation, take off the linen garments that he had put on when he went into the holy place, and leave them there. Aaron shall bathe with water in the holy place then put on his garments. He shall come out, offer his burnt offering, and the burnt offering of the people. Then, Aaron shall make atonement for himself and for the people. Aaron shall burn the fat of the sin offering on the altar. The man who released the scapegoat shall wash his clothes, bathe in water, and then come into the camp. The bull and goat for the sin offerings must be taken outside the camp. The blood from these animals must be brought in for the atonement of the holy place. The bull of the sin offering and the goat for the sin offering shall be carried out the camp and burned. Also, their skins, flesh, and intestines shall be burned in the fire. Leviticus 16: 20-27

The significance of the scapegoat to Jesus is this: Jesus bore the sins of the people of the world as the scapegoat bore the sins of Israel. Although Jesus died, he was resurrected. Jesus, therefore, in a sense was both the Scapegoat and the Sacrificial Lamb of God.

• Leprosy, Sacrifice, and the Scapegoat

There are parallels in the typologies of the priestly ceremony of healing leprosy, the rituals of blood sacrifices, and the ceremony of the scapegoat. These things relate to us in that Jesus freed us from the attachment of sins.

This shall be the law of the leper in the day of his cleansing. He shall be brought to the priest. The priest shall go out of the camp and look to see if the leper is healed of the plague of leprosy. Then shall the priest command that the leper get two living clean birds, cedar wood, a scarlet cord, and hyssop branches. These things are for the cleansing of leprosy. The priest shall order one of the birds killed in a clay bowl over running water. As for the living bird, he shall take it, the cedar wood, the scarlet cord, the hyssop branches, and dip them in the blood of the bird that was killed over the running water. The priest shall sprinkle the blood seven times on the person who is to be cleansed of leprosy. The priest shall pronounce that the person who had leprosy is clean. **Then the priest shall let the living bird loose into the open field.** *Leviticus 14:1-7*

- **Attaching no Strings**

Jesus is a type of several biblical elements of sacrifices and redemptions.

  A. Jesus as the goat for the sin offerings; **redeems**.

  B. Jesus as the scapegoat for the sin offerings; **releaes**.

  C. Jesus as the sacrificial lamb for the sin offerings; **relieves**.

  D. Jesus as our High Priest for the sin offerings; **frees**.

Therefore, Jesus sacrificial death and redemptive role gave us unconditional relationships to God **with no strings attached**.

PRINCIPLE AND PRACTICE SEVEN
Overflowing Cups

By faith Isaac blessed Jacob and Esau concerning things to come. Hebrews 11:20

Genesis 25:19-26 give pertinent information regarding the circumstances of the birth of Jacob and Esau. They were twin sons of Isaac and Rebekah. Rebekah had been unable to have children. Isaac prayed to God concerning Rebekah's infertility. As a result, Rebekah became pregnant with Esau and Jacob. The babies struggled against each other within Rebekah's womb. So, she asked God the meaning of the struggle. The Lord told her that each son would be a founder of a great nation. The rivalry continued during birth. Esau was born first with Jacob holding on to his heel. Thus, the name Jacob means "supplanter." That is, someone who "displaces" or "trips" another person.

Accordingly, when they became adults, Jacob tricked Esau on two occasions. On the first occasion, Jacob tricked Esau into selling his rights as a first-born son to him.

The boys grew up. Esau was a cunning hunter and a man of the field. Jacob was a quiet man who stayed among the tents. Isaac loved Esau. Esau hunted wild animals that Isaac enjoyed eating. But, Rebekah loved Jacob. Once, when Jacob was cooking red bean soup, Esau came in exhausted from the field. Esau said to Jacob, "I beg you, give me some of your red bean soup. I am weak from hunger." So, people called Esau, Edom. [The Hebrew word Edom sounds like the word red]. Jacob responded, "Today, sell me your rights of a first-born son." Esau said, "Look, I am at the point of dying. What good

*is my birthright to me if I am dead?"
Jacob insisted, "Make a vow to me
now." Esau made a vow and sold his
birthright to Jacob. Then Jacob gave
Esau bread and the red bean soup.
Esau ate and drank, rose up, and went
his way. This was how much Esau cared
about his birthright. Genesis 25:27-34*

The second event of trickery by Jacob perpetrated on Esau is in Genesis 27:1-40. The plot started in Genesis 27:1-10 when Isaac asked Esau to prepare a favorite dish. Isaac intended to pronounce paternal blessings on Esau after eating the meal. Rebekah overheard the conversation between Isaac and Esau. So, when Esau went to hunt, Rebekah told Jacob what Isaac told Esau. Rebecca instructed Jacob to go to the flock and select two fat young goats so that she could cook them for Isaac. Rebekah told Jacob that he could take the food to Isaac and receive his father's blessings before he died. Isaac was old and unable to see well. Some very intriguing events followed as

Principles of Belief and Practices of Faith

Jacob conspired to deceive his father and defraud his brother.

> *Jacob said to his mother Rebekah, "Look, Esau my brother is a hairy man, and I am a smooth man. If my father touches me, he will know that he is being deceived and this will bring a curse on me, and not a blessing." His mother said to him, "On me be your curse, my son, just do what I say." Jacob got the goats and brought them to his mother. Rebekah cooked the meat just as Isaac loved it. Then, she took the best clothes of her eldest son Esau that were in the house and put them on Jacob her younger son. She put the skins of young goats on his hands and on the smooth parts of his neck. Lastly, Rebekah gave the tasty meat and the bread that she had prepared to Jacob. Jacob went to his father and said, "My father!" Isaac replied, "Here am I. Who are you, my son?" Jacob said*

262

to his father, "I am Esau your first-born. I have done what you asked me. Please sit and eat my meat so that you may bless me. Isaac asked, "How is it that you hunted so quickly, my son?" Jacob replied, "Because the Lord your God brought the animal to me." Isaac said, "Come near that I may feel you my son. This way I will know whether you are really my son Esau. Jacob went near to Isaac. Isaac said, "The voice is Jacob's voice, but the hands are the hands of Esau." Isaac did not know that he was Jacob because his hands were hairy like Esau's hands. So, Isaac blessed Jacob. After that, Isaac asked, "Are you really my son Esau?" Jacob replied, "I am." Isaac said, "Bring the food near to me. I will eat of my son's meat so that my soul may bless you." Jacob brought the food to Isaac and he ate it. Jacob also brought Isaac wine and he drank it. Isaac said to Jacob, "Come near now, and kiss me, my son." Jacob came near and kissed him. Isaac smelled the clothes that Jacob wore, blessed him, and said, "See, the smell of my son is as the smell of a field which the Lord has blessed." Genesis 27:11-27.

Isaac, having been deceived, powerfully blessed Jacob. He said,

"Therefore, may God give you much rain, fertile soil, an abundance of corn, and wine. May people serve you and nations bow down to you. May you rule over your relatives. May your descendants bow down to you. Let everyone who curses you be cursed. Let everyone who blesses you be blessed." Genesis 27:28-29

Later, in a deeply moving episode Esau also is blessed.

As soon as Isaac finished blessing Jacob, Esau came in from hunting. Esau

also had made a tasty meal of meat. He brought it to his father and said, "Let my father arise and eat his son's meat so that he may bless me." Isaac inquired of Esau, "Who are you?" Esau answered, "I am your son, your eldest son, Esau." Isaac trembled excessively and said, "Who? Where is the person who killed an animal and brought it me? I ate all of the meat before you came, and I blessed him. Indeed, he shall be blessed." When Esau heard the words of his father, he cried with a great and exceedingly bitter scream and said to his father, "Bless me, even me also, oh my father." Isaac said, "Your brother came cunningly and took your blessing." Esau said, "Is he not correctly named Jacob? He has supplanted me two times. He took away my birthright, and look, now he has taken away my blessing." Then Esau said to his father, "Have you reserved a blessing for me?" Isaac answered, "Indeed, I have made

Jacob your ruler. I have given him all his brothers to be his servants. I have blessed him with corn and wine. What else is there for me to give you, my son?" Then Esau said to his father, "Do you not have but one blessing for me, my father? Bless me also, my father." Esau raised his voice and wept. Isaac said, "Look, you shall not live on fertile land and be blessed by rain. You shall live by your sword and serve your brother. <u>Eventually, you shall have the power to break his yoke from off your neck."</u> Genesis 27:30-40

Esau was determined to kill Jacob after Isaac died, so Rebekah convinced Isaac to send Jacob to Haran, a city in northern Mesopotamia, to choose a wife from her brother's daughters. Rebekah's brother name was Laban. Also, Laban was Abraham's nephew (see Genesis 22:20-24). Indeed, Isaac passed on to Jacob the promised blessings of Abraham.

Overflowing Cups

Isaac called Jacob, blessed and charged him saying, "You shall not take a wife of the daughters of Canaan. Arise, go to Padanaram, to the house of Bethuel your mother's father and take a wife from the daughters of Laban, your mother's brother. May God Almighty bless you, make you have many children and multiply your descendants. May God bless you with many descendants and give you the blessing of Abraham. May God bless your descendants so that you inherit the land where you are a foreigner; the same land that He gave Abraham." Then Isaac sent Jacob away. Jacob went to Padanaram, to Laban, the son of Bethuel the Syrian, the brother of Rebekah, Jacob's and Esau's mother. Genesis 28:1-5

In contrast, Esau married into his uncle Ishmael's family.

Esau seeing that the daughters of Canaan did not please Isaac, his father, he went to Ishmael and took other wives. He married Mahalath the daughter of Ishmael, Abraham's son. Genesis 28: 8-9

• Inviting dishonesty

Jacob spent twenty years at Laban's house in Haran. First, he served seven years under contract as an indentured servant in order to marry Laban's youngest daughter, Rachel. But, after the contract was fulfilled, Laban tricked Jacob into marrying Rachel's older sister, Leah (see Genesis 29:15-30). Laban's explanation of the deceit was, "The custom in our country does not allow the younger daughter to marry before the eldest daughter" (Genesis 29:26).

Jacob had to work seven more years to marry Rachel. Moreover, in Genesis 31:41, Jacob complained that he had to work six additional years to earn animals from Laban and during that time he changed Jacob's wages ten times.

Possibly, Laban's statement to Jacob in Genesis 29:15, "Because you are my brother, should you therefore work for me for nothing? Tell me, what shall your wages be?" meant more than accommodating a relative. Apparently, Laban had no sons at the time. According to some customs of the time, Jacob was for all practical purposes, Laban's heir. This might explain Laban's manipulation of Jacob's rights.

Jacob received his blessings through trickery. Consequently, he himself was tricked and had to work hard to keep his blessings. Dishonesty invites more dishonesty. True blessings don't come by being deceitful. Once we are blessed through deceit, we have to keep deceiving others in order to keep our blessings. We should not want to be blessed by other people's misery. We should not be blessed and worry about keeping our blessings. We should not have to be constantly looking over our shoulders because of our blessings.

In order for Jacob to free himself of Laban, Jacob again used trickery (see Genesis 30:25-43). Jacob's contention was that God had blessed

Laban mightily. Jacob further argued that those blessings came through him by working for Laban. Jacob said that it was time for him to acquire some security for his family. He refused an offer of wages from Laban. Instead, Jacob made a proposal to Laban.

> *Jacob said, "Let me go through all your flock today, removing from it every speckled and spotted sheep and every black lamb. Let me do the same with the goats; and such shall be my wages. So, in the future you will know that I am honest. When you come and find only speckled and spotted among my animals." Genesis 30:32-33*

Jacob cut green branches from poplar, almond, and plane trees. Next, Jacob peeled some of the bark from the trees so that the branches had white stripes on them. Then he put the branches in front of the animals at the watering places. At times when the flocks came to drink, they also mated there. Therefore, when the goats mated in front of the branches they produced young animals that were born streaked, speckled, or spotted. Jacob separated the goats from the sheep. He made them mate with the streaked and black animals from Laban's flock. Jacob put the branches in front of the stronger animals in the flock when they were mating. He didn't do the same when the weaker animals mated. Consequently, the animals born from the weaker animals were Laban's but the animals born from the stronger animals belonged to Jacob. As a result, Jacob became very wealthy.

In addition to fact that Jacob wanted to leave Laban, there were at least five factors that made Jacob decide to get away secretly from his father-in-law. First, by this time, Laban had sons. They realized that Jacob as heir to Laban, while he remained at Laban's house in the status of an adopted son, presented a problem for them (the custom of the time most likely regarded Jacob as an adopted son when Laban had no heir). Second, apart from a presumed right to inheritance that Jacob had in the family, the newly acquired wealth of Jacob presented more problems for Laban's sons. Third, Laban's attitude toward Jacob changed. Fourth, God told Jacob to leave and return the land of his ancestors and family. Fifth, God promised to be with him (see Genesis 31:1-3).

Jacob reasoned that God blessed him with the cattle bred from Laban's flock because Laban had been unscrupulous to him many times. Jacob said that God spoke to him in a dream about the manner in which he mated the animals. God also reminded Jacob that he was the same God who previously revealed Himself to him at Bethel (see Genesis 31:4-13).

• The Transcendences of Belief and Faith

There is definitely a movement of transcendences in the cycle of Jacob's life. God revealed Himself to Jacob progressively through imageries and epiphanies. These events were apart and independent of ordinary human and other physical occurrences. They moved Jacob to experience God from "a god is somewhere," to "God is out there," to "God is around here," to "God is here," to "God surrounds here," to "God is right here," and finally to "God is in here."

Immanent

I call Jacob's first experience of the transcendence of God, "immanent." This happened on his way to Haran as he escaped the rage of his brother Esau. It was Jacob's basic understanding of the otherworldliness of God through His permanent existence and operation in the universe. This revelation of the immanence of God was "a god is somewhere."

Jacob left Beersheba and went toward Haran. He stopped at a certain place because the sun was setting. Jacob stayed there all night. He took stones from that place and made pillows of them. He laid down and slept there.

Jacob dreamt that he saw a ladder resting on the ground with the top of it reaching into the sky. He saw angels of God ascending and descending on it. The Lord stood above the ladder and said, "I am the Lord God of Abraham your father and the God of Isaac. The land where you lie, I will give you and your descendants. Your descendants shall be as the dust of the earth. They shall spread abroad to the west, to the east, to the north, and to the south. Through you and your descendants shall all the families of the earth be blessed. Be aware, I am with you and will protect you wherever you go. I will bring you again to this land because I will not leave you until I have done what I have promised you." Genesis 28:10-15*

Notice that God gave Jacob the same promise that He gave his father, Isaac, and his grandfather, Abraham.

Eminent

Another experience of Jacob with God was "eminent." This was part of Jacob's encounter with God on his way to Haran. This revelation of God's eminence was the realization that "God is out there" and we can clearly see Him as superior to all creation.

Jacob awoke from his sleep and he said, "<u>Surely the Lord is in this place and I knew it not</u>." He was afraid and said, "This is a frightful place! This is none other but the house of God and the gate of heaven." Jacob rose up early in the morning. He took the stone that he had put for his pillows, set it up for a pillar, and poured oil on top of it. He called the name of that place Bethel [The house of God]. Formerly, the name of that city was Luz. Genesis 28:16-19

Imminent

Jacob realized that God is close to human events when he experienced God by feeling that something out of the ordinary was about to happen. This encounter happened as he fled from the rage of his father-in-law Laban. This event of imminence I term, "God is around here."

> Then Jacob rose up, and put his sons and his wives on camels. He carried away all his cattle, and all his goods that he had gotten in Padanaram to go to Isaac, his father, in Canaan, while Laban went to shear his sheep. In the meantime, <u>Rachel stole the images that belonged to her father</u>. So, Jacob stole away unawares to Laban, the Syrian, in that he did not tell him that he was leaving. Therefore, he fled with all that he owned. He rose, passed over the river, and went toward Mount Gilead. Three days later, Laban was told that Jacob had fled. Laban took

his relatives with him and pursued Jacob for seven days. They caught up to Jacob at Mount Gilead. At night, God came to Laban in a dream and said to him, "Be careful. Do not say anything to Jacob, good or bad." Eventually, Laban overtook Jacob. Now, Jacob had pitched his tent in the hills, so Laban with his relatives pitched their tents on Mount Gilead. Laban said to Jacob, "What have you done? Have you stolen away unawares to me and carried away my daughters as captives taken in war? Why did you flee secretly and did not tell me? I might have sent you away with mirth, with singings, and the playing of tambourines and harp. You did not allow me to kiss my sons and my daughters. In so doing, now you have done foolishly. It is in my power to hurt you. However, the God of your father spoke to me last night saying, 'Be careful not to speak to Jacob either good or bad.' Now, even though *you needed to go, because you longed to go back to your father's house, <u>still, why have you stolen my gods?</u>" Jacob answered, "Because I was afraid. I said to myself, perhaps you might take your daughters from me by force." Genesis 31: 17 -31*

Jacob did not steal the Teraphim but it was likely that he knew that Rachel did. Part of Laban's rage probably involved the facts that Jacob may have felt that he had rights to the household gods because Laban abused him by possibly claiming him as heir and now he was married to two of his daughters. Perhaps, these might be the reasons why God warned Laban to be careful how he spoke to Jacob. At any rate, as idol worshippers they believed that it was necessary to take their gods with them. Jacob felt that God was about to do something yet he still needed the protection of idol statuettes. God's transcendence of imminence revealed to Jacob that he didn't need to carry gods with him. God was around him.

Immense

In spite of having been cheated of his birth-right and inheritance, Esau eventually acquired wealth and power. This revealed the "immensity of God." Therefore, later as Jacob traveled south away from Laban, Jacob recognized that God was with him in an immense way as he called a place along the way, Mahanaim. This meant that there was a camp for him and a camp for God there.

Jacob, passing near Esau's territory, remembered that Esau had threatened to kill him. Therefore, Jacob decided to appease Esau with yet another trick. He sent messengers to Esau calling himself Esau's servant. Jacob's intention was to make Esau know that he was wealthy and did not need the inheritance that he stole from him. The messengers returned with news that Jacob did not want to hear. Esau was on his way with 400 men.

Jacob panicked. He was convinced that Esau was coming to destroy him. He divided the people and animals into two camps hoping that at least one camp would survive. Then,

Jacob prayed. He acknowledged God to be the God of his grandfather Abraham and his father Isaac. He bargained that God blessed him substantially to that point in his life in spite of his unworthiness. Furthermore, God had directed him to go back home to his relatives and promised him more prosperity. He begged God to save him and his family from the power of Esau. He further bargained with God that He had given him the same promise given to Abraham and Isaac, that his generations will be numerous and prosperous.

Jacob did two things that indicated that he was still not totally relying on God. First, when he divided his people and assets into two camps, he forgot that he had previously designated a camp for God. Why not put everybody and everything in God's camp.

Second, after praying to God he still devised another scheme to trick Esau. He purposely selected a significant amount of animals as gifts for Esau. Then he divided the animals into groups. Later, he sent a servant ahead with each group with a distance between them.

Overflowing Cups

Therefore, every few miles Esau met a servant from Jacob with presents, each time referring to Jacob as servant and Esau as master. Jacob's plan was to "cover Esau's face." Jacob said when "I see Esau's face" maybe he will "lift up my face." Jacob did not consider that trying to appease Esau this way might further enrage him. After all, Esau might realize that he was being tricked again (see Genesis 32:1-23).

Jacob was restless that night. So he sent his family and possessions across the Jabbock River.

Jacob was left alone. There he wrestled with a man until daybreak. When the man saw that he did not prevail against Jacob, he struck the socket of Jacob's hip, as he wrestled with him, so that it came out of the joint. The man said, "Let me go because the sun is rising." Jacob said, "I will not let you go until you bless me." The man asked Jacob, "What is your name?" He answered, "Jacob!" Then the man said, your name will be Jacob no longer. Your name will be Israel because you have struggled with God and with humans and survived (the word Israel could mean among other things to struggle or to strive with God). Jacob said to him, "Tell me, I implore you, your name." The man asked. "Why do you ask my name?" The man blessed Jacob there. Jacob called the name of the place Peniel. Jacob said, "Because I have seen God face to face and my life was spared" (Peniel means the face of God). As Jacob was leaving Peniel the sun came up. He was limping because of his hip. Genesis 32: 24-31

When Esau met with Jacob, it created a sense of "God is here."

Jacob lifted up his eyes, and looked, and saw Esau coming with four hundred men. So, he divided the children among Leah, Rachel, and two maids.

Overflowing Cups

He put the maids and their children ahead, Leah and her children after, and Rachel and Joseph last. He went ahead of them and bowed down to the ground seven times, until he came near to his brother. Esau ran to meet him, embraced him, fell on his neck, kissed him, and they wept. Esau lifted up his eyes, saw the women and the children, and inquired, "Who are these with you?" Jacob replied, "The children who God graciously gave your servant." Then the maids came near with their children and bowed down. Leah also with her children came near and bowed down. After, Joseph and Rachel came near and they bowed down. Esau said, "I saw many herds as I came. What does this mean?" Jacob explained, "These are to find favor with you my lord." Esau said, "I have enough my brother, keep what you have." Jacob said, "No, please if now I have found grace in your sight, then accept my presents because now that I see your face, it is as though I see the face of God, and you are pleased with me." Genesis 33:1-10

Immutable

God's purpose never changes. Therefore, His will to bless never changes. Esau appearing with many blessings underscored this reality. Esau eventually accepted Jacob's gifts. This was important to Jacob as an act of atonement. For Jacob, finding "grace in Esau's sight" was a sense of "God surrounds here."

Jacob said "Please take my blessings that I bring to you because God has been gracious to me and I have enough." Because Jacob begged so much, Esau took the gifts. Then Esau said, "Let us take our journey. I will go ahead of you." Jacob said to him, "My lord you know that the children are weak, and among the flocks and herds are young animals. If the men should

drive them hard one day, all the flocks will die. Please, let my lord go ahead of his servant, and I will follow as quickly as I can and meet you in Edom." Esau said, "Let me leave with you some of my men." Jacob said, "Thanks, but there is no need to do that. I only want to find grace in the sight of my lord."
Genesis 33:11-15

Immediate

Jacob did not go with Esau to Seir (Edom). He went to Succoth - a place of "shelter." For Jacob, this meant, "God is right here." God was his shelter. He then realized that he could totally depend on God. There was nothing that stood between him and God. God was "immediate." Therefore, Jacob no longer needed to "play tricks."

So, Esau returned that day on his way to Seir. <u>Jacob journeyed to Succoth, built a house, and made booths for his cattle. Therefore the name of the place</u>

285

is called Succoth (Succoth means shel-ter). Genesis 33:16-17

Immanuel

For Jacob, the unique experience of Imman-uel (with us is God) is "God is in here." This came about because Jacob was fleeing once again. Genesis 33:18-19 tell us that after some time Jacob went back to Canaan. Thus, God ful-filled His promise stated in Genesis 28:15. The place that he came to was Shechem where he bought land. Jacob set up an altar there that he called "Powerful is the God of Israel." This in-dicated that by then Jacob could publicly de-clare that the God of Abraham and Isaac was also his God. This was a very discernable pro-gression from his "immanent experience" with God and not one of "bargaining with God." This contrast is shown in Genesis 28:16-22.

After some time, a man named Shechem forc-ibly raped Jacob's daughter, Dinah. Shechem wanted to marry Dinah. Part of the reason for this was to acquire some of the wealth of the Israelites. Jacob's sons felt deceived by their neighbors. They did not want to be absorbed into the Canaanites through marriage. Instead, they deceivingly proposed that all the men of the city be circumcised so that Dinah could marry Shechem. While the men were sore and in pain from the circumcision, Simeon and Levi, full brothers of Dinah through their mother, Leah, killed all the males of Shechem, including Shechem himself. Those events led to Jacob's flight with his family (see Genesis 34:1-31).

God said to Jacob, "Arise, go up to Bethel and dwell there. Make an altar there for God, who appeared to you when you fled from the face of Esau your brother." Then Jacob said to his family, and to all others who were with him, "Put away the strange gods that are among you, and be clean, and change your garments. Let us arise, and go up to Bethel. I will make an altar there for God who answered me in the day of my distress and was with me in the way that I went." They gave Jacob all the strange gods that they had, and all their earrings which were in their ears. Jacob hid them under the oak tree near Shechem. When they left there, God made the people of the nearby cities afraid so that they did not pursue the sons of Jacob. So, Jacob and all the people who were with him came to Luz, which is in the land of Canaan, that is, Bethel. Jacob built an altar there. He called the place Elbethel because God appeared to him there when he fled from the face of his brother (Elbethel means the God of Bethel). But, Deborah, Rebekah's nurse died and she was buried at Bethel under an oak tree. The place was named Allonbachuth (Allonbachuth means the oak of weeping). God appeared to Jacob again, when he came out of Padanaram, and blessed him. God said to him, "Your name is Jacob but your name shall not be Jacob any more. Israel shall be your name. God called him Israel. God said to Israel, "I am God Almighty. Be fruitful and multiply. A nation and a company of nations shall come from you. Kings shall be your descendants. The land that I gave Abraham and Isaac, I will give you and your descendants." God left him. Then, Jacob set up a pillar of stone where he talked with God. He poured a drink of offering and oil on the place. Jacob named the place Bethel. Genesis 35:1-15

Jacob's Immanuel transcendent experience with God revealed something deeper than imminence. That is, in addition to not needing to take gods with him, he could get rid of the ones that he had with him. This experience also was a prototype of the following familiar prophecy:

Therefore, the Lord himself shall give you a sign. "Look, a virgin shall conceive, bear a son, and shall call his name Immanuel." Isaiah 7:14

The above prophecy is generally accepted as messianic. It predicts the birth of Jesus. Jacob's Immanuel transcendent experience was therefore a foreshadowing of the coming of Jesus that led eventually to the indwelling Spirit in us. Jesus said in John 14:16-17,

> *I will pray that the Father give you another Helper who will abide with you forever. He is the Spirit of Truth who the world cannot receive, because it does not see Him or know Him. But, you know Him because He dwells with you, and shall be in you.*

• **Overflowing Cups**

Because of the various perspectives of Esau and Jacob's relationships to God in this chapter, I see three elements to the Principle and

Overflowing Cups

Practice of Overflowing Cups. They are: *Things to Come, Facing Realities, and the Face of God.*

Things to Come

Isaac blessed both Jacob and Esau. This was in spite of Jacob defrauding Esau of his birthright and cheating him of their father's final blessings. In fact, Isaac confidently expressed that Esau would be blessed also. This action was the faith of Isaac in terms of the "things to come" of Hebrews 11:20. Therefore, although we make mistakes our acts of faith can still bring about great results.

Moreover, even though our dreams, desires, and aspirations may dry up in front of our faces, we should not lose hope in God. Notwithstanding missed opportunities, we should avoid thinking, "I could have or I should have." When we miss our boats, God can provide us with rocket ships.

Furthermore, we sometimes become disenchanted and disheartened when we do good things for others and they do not appreciate the blessings that they receive through us.

Often, we feel used and abused, as well as, foolish because people take advantage of our kindness. These are issues for many Christians.

In addition, many people often trick believers into helping them. They prey on our generosity. Actually, they count on our benevolence to help them defraud us. Therefore, they frequently say things such as "the church is supposed to help people or since you are a Christian you're supposed to help us." This can upset us.

However, if we truly believe that we are blessed by God and that we are instruments and conduits of his blessings, then we should know that God's blessings through us are not wasted ever on anyone. Many times, even when people misuse our blessings, others are still blessed through them. For example, not everyone who goes to a food pantry of a church is a person in need of that ministry. Yet, they sometimes share their food with others who are hungry.

Facing Realities

There are references to the words *face* and *eyes* as well as many phrases relating to *face or eyes* that are in the events surrounding Jacob's encounter with Esau (see Genesis 32: 1-32 and 33: 1-11).

In Genesis 32:5 Jacob wanted to find favor in Esau's *eyes*.

In Genesis 32:20 Jacob wanted to appease (to hide) Esau's *face* with gifts.

In Genesis 32:20 Jacob wanted to see Esau's *face* (to be favorable) to him.

In Genesis 32:20 Jacob wanted Esau to lift up his (Jacob's) *face* (to forgive Jacob).

In Genesis 32:30 Jacob named the place that he wrestled with a man all night *Peniel* (the *face* of God).

In Genesis 32:30 Jacob said that he saw God *face* to *face* when he wrestled with the man all night.

In Genesis 33:1 Jacob *lifted up his eyes to see* Esau.

In Genesis 33:5 Esau *lifted up his eyes and saw* Jacob's family.

In Genesis 33:8 Jacob explained that he wanted to find favor in the *eyes* of Esau by offering him presents.

In Genesis 33:10 Jacob insisted that Esau take his presents so that Jacob may find favor in Esau's *eyes*.

In Genesis 33:10 Jacob said that he saw the *face* of Esau.

In Genesis 33:10 Jacob stated that when he saw Esau's *face* it was like *seeing* the *face* of God.

The reality was that Jacob eventually had to *face* was not just that he was the younger son. It was also that he did not have to be a trickster to succeed. God had a purpose for Jacob's life even though he was not the elder son. Wealth and power would have been included in that purpose. In order to be fully blessed, we must *face realities*. God intends for us to be who we are. He will not bless us for trying to be another person. He will not give us blessings that are intended for someone else.

Overflowing Cups

Moreover, God blesses us all. We should not compare our blessings with others who we believe are more blessed than us. Otherwise, we might spend a lifetime time trying to get what God never intended for us to have in the first place. Being true to ourselves is being true to God.

If we are tricksters, people will know this. If we are not true to ourselves, people will know this too. God had been talking to Jacob all along. Every transcendent experience that Jacob had proves this. Likewise, God talks to the sincerity of our hearts. What might be your transcendent experiences with God?

Jacob spent many years trying to be first in his family's order of inheritance that he might be blessed. But, when he encountered Esau who he had tricked to get ahead of in life, the reality of being first and being blessed struck him. We are truly blessed regardless of our positions in life when we put God first. In referring to material blessings, Jesus said in Matthew 6:33 "Seek <u>first</u> the kingdom of God and his righteousness and all these things shall be given to you." Being first with God is to give God our best. Indeed, it is to give God our first. This is explained in the Principle of Belief and the Practice of Faith One. There is a tendency for people to admire a Jacob type person in that he was aggressive. Spunk and initiative are admired qualities among us. And, sometimes I wonder whether society as a whole is becoming more aggressive in many ways. For instance, one can see the "getting ahead of others regardless" attitude with what appears to be more and more people driving cars aggressively these days.

The face of God

Jacob saw God in Esau's face. Often, our true relationship with God is found in the "face" of another person. This is what I call the "God, you, and I connection." This is well illustrated in Jesus' parable in Matthew 25:31-41. Jesus said:

> *"When the Son of Man comes in His glory, and all the holy angels with*

Overflowing Cups

Him, then shall He sit on the throne of His glory. Before Him shall be gathered all nations and He shall separate them from each other as a shepherd divides his sheep from the goats. He shall put the sheep on His right hand, but the goats on the left. Then shall the King say to them on His right hand, 'Come, and be blessed by the Father. Inherit the kingdom prepared for you from the beginning of the world. Because, I was hungry, and you gave me food; I was thirsty, and you gave me drink; I was a stranger, and you took me in; I was naked, and you clothed me; I was sick, and you visited me; I was in prison, and you visited me.' Then shall the righteous answer him saying, 'Lord, when did we see you hungry and fed you? Or thirsty, and gave you drink? When were you a stranger and we took you in, or naked, and clothed you? Or, when were you sick, or in prison, and we came to visit you?' The King shall answer, 'Truly, I tell you, seeing that you have done this to one of the least of my brothers, you have done it to me.' Then shall He say also to them on the left hand, 'Depart from Me, you are condemned to the everlasting fire that is prepared for the devil and his angels.'"

Jacob saw the face of God when he wrestled with the man. Then he saw the face of God in Esau's face. These were perceptions of relating to God that Jacob never had before.

Similarly, we can see the face of God in others when we respond to their needs. Responding to the needs of others shows that we are struggling with our own need to relate to God as we strive with Him.

In the familiar verse below, "overflows" literally means to make fat.

You prepare a table before me and in the presence of my enemies. You anoint my head with oil; my cup <u>overflows</u>. Psalm 23:5

Overflowing Cups

In the final analysis, overflowing cups (making fat) means three things. First, God blessings are always sufficient. Second, God's blessings are always more than we need. Third, God's blessings are always more than enough.

Our blessings, anyhow, generally come through others. And, the good thing about it is that God does not have to take away blessings from some people to give to others in order for them to be blessed. Therefore, *God blessings are always sufficient.*

The blessings weren't really Isaac to give but God's. The eldest son's blessings would be for the benefit of the entire family. Consequently, *God's blessings are always more than we need.*

From human perspectives, Isaac's blessings were limited through tradition to the eldest son. Since it appears that Esau became more rich and powerful than Jacob did, then ultimately *God's blessings are always more than enough.*

For many of us, we often feel that we have been cheated literally from birth. We often feel that we are always in the wrong place at the wrong time or even the right time, for that matter. We often feel that opportunities have passed us up. Could these feelings be related to the following questions?

> Have you ever been cheated of any-thing?
> Has anyone taken from you what you thought should have been yours?
> Even after you have prayed for some-thing, has anyone lied to you or mis-led you?

How many of us after waiting and antici-pating blessings that we have prayed for have been devastated when we see the blessings going to someone else? By the way, those blessings weren't for us anyway. We won't feel cheated if we understand the element of God's blessings of *in the meantime of our faith* found in the Principle of Belief and Practice of Faith Three. This element teaches us to trust God regardless how much the circumstances

Overflowing Cups

of blessings seem to be working against us. If we trust God long enough, our cups will over-flow. This is definitely illustrated by the story of Esau and Jacob.

PRINCIPLE AND PRACTICE EIGHT
Claiming our Inheritance

By faith Jacob, when he was a dying, blessed both the sons of Joseph; and worshipped, leaning on the top of his staff. Hebrews 11:21

The story of Joseph, the son of Jacob, is in Genesis chapters 30 through 50. Hebrews 11:21 is specifically referring to the incident below.

> *Someone told Joseph, "Your father is sick." Joseph went with his two sons, Manasseh and Ephraim, to see his father. Someone else told Jacob, "Look, your son Joseph comes to see you." Israel strengthened himself, and sat on the bed. Jacob said to Joseph, "God Almighty appeared to me at Luz in the*

land of Canaan and blessed me. He said to me, "I will make you have many children, and you will have many descendants. I will give this land to your descendants for all times. Now your two sons, Ephraim and Manasseh, who were born to you in the land of Egypt before I came to you there, as Reuben and Simeon, they are mine. If you have other children, they shall be yours, and they shall be recorded under the names of their brothers in matters of their inheritance. Genesis 48:1-6

There were twelve tribes of Israel. Ten sons of Jacob became heads of tribes. Therefore, Jacob was leaning on the Lord for guidance when he blessed Manasseh and Ephraim. They were not Jacob's son. They were his grandsons, Joseph's sons. That meant that Jacob passed on to his grandsons, Manasseh and Ephraim, the blessings of becoming heads of tribes.

Claiming our Inheritance

Before the years of famine came, two sons were born to Joseph and Asenath the daughter of Potipherah, priest of On. Joseph named the first-born Manasseh. He said, "Because God made me forget all my toil, and my father's household" (the word Manasseh sounds like the word in Hebrew for cause to forget). Joseph named the second son Ephraim. He said, "Because God caused me to have children in the land of my affliction" (the word Ephraim sounds like the word in Hebrew for cause to have children). Genesis 41:50-52

God's blessings are *extensive* in that they reached to Joseph's children. As we are being blessed our children and descendants are being blessed also - even those who are not born yet. This is the essence of God's promise to Abraham, his descendants, and us.

As I wrote previously in this book, we can connect the image the Lord being our Shepherd of Psalm 23 to us living successfully. Specifically, verse four of Psalm 23 shows how depending on God blesses us and our descendants.

> *Although I walk through the valley of the shadow of death, I will fear no evil, because You are with me; Your <u>rod</u> and Your <u>staff,</u> they comfort me. Psalm 23:4*

The rod and the staff are comparable to a king's scepter. They show authority (see Exodus 4:1-5, 7:9-13). This kind of authority can be typed to Jacob's staff in the eleventh chapter of Hebrews. Definitely, Jacob acted with authority when he blessed his grandsons.

The staff in the above scripture reference also indicates dependency on God. Shepherds were known to lean on staffs as they stood for long periods watching their sheep. Jacob certainly needed the staff for support.

Taking the rod and staff as a single unit, the curved part of the staff was known to be used by shepherds to gentle bring stray sheep back into the flock. Shepherds used the straight rod as a weapon to defend the sheep against wild animals.

The rod and the staff in Psalm 23 tell us that even when we are near death we can be confident of the legacy of God's blessings. Actually, throughout our lives we should lean (depend) on the Lord and not on our own understanding:

> Trust in the Lord with all your heart and _lean_ not to your own understanding. In all your ways acknowledge Him and He shall direct your paths. Proverbs 3:5-6

If we walk by faith and not by sight, then we walk by God's guidance. I don't believe literally in "blind faith." I believe that faith is purposeful and deliberate. Therefore, if we don't depend on ourselves when we walk in faith, then God becomes our walking sticks (staffs).

• **Worship and Faith**

As Jacob leaned on his staff, he worshipped God. Worship is connected to faith in that both depict acts of confidence in God. However, Jacob was weak with age but he "strengthened himself" when supporting himself with the staff. The act "strengthened himself" portrayed affirmation in God that went beyond confidence. Actually, we can contrast his worship and faith with his physical weakness and age. As recorded in John 4:23-24 concerning worship, it is not a physical place or condition, it is a relationship of spirit and truth with God. As recorded in Matthew 17:19-20 concerning a mustard seed, its tree, and the size of a mountain, faith is not about our age or strength. On the contrary, the power of faith is relative and extensive.

• **Legacy and Faith**

Legacy generally means that which is inherited or handed down from previous generations. We share our blessings with others while we are alive. But, true believers make provisions for others to receive our blessings after we die. The Principle of the Belief and the Practice of Faith of Claiming our Inheritance demands that we exercise stewardship to our families, churches, and worthwhile causes through legacy. Obviously, our lives in Christ are testimonies and legacies for others. Indeed, the lives of the people mentioned in chapter eleven of Hebrews serve as legacies of faith to all who followed including us today.

The Principle Belief and Practice of Faith of Claiming our Inheritance as illustrated in Hebrews 11:21 underscores that the biblical people of faith really lived with expectations for us so we should live with expectations of those who come behind us.

• **Inheritance and Faith**

There are two fundamentals about inheritance in this Principle of Belief and Practice of Faith. They are *justification* and *adoption*. This is apparent in Ephesians 1:1-23. In this passage, we find that God blessed us in terms of a legacy through Jesus Christ even before the creation of the world. All our blessings are in "heavenly places" to be claimed by us as our inheritance. We are justified and adopted into God's family through the redemptive acts of faith by Jesus' sacrificial death. Adoption, in New Testament times meant full acceptance into a family. This was certified through legal proceedings by a document of justification. Therefore, you are fully entitled to your inheritance. Go ahead, claim it. Claim all of it!

PRINCIPLE AND PRACTICE NINE
Looking to the Future

By faith Joseph, when he was dying, spoke of the Hebrew people leaving Egypt and gave them instructions concerning his burial. Hebrews 11:22

Hebrews 11:22 is referring to a passage of Scripture found in Genesis 50: 22-26.

> *Joseph continued to live in Egypt with his father's family. Joseph lived there until he died when he was one hundred and ten years old. Joseph lived to see Ephraim's children and grandchildren. Also, Joseph brought up the children of Machir, the son of Manasseh, as his own. Joseph said to his brothers, "I am about to die but God will be with you. He will take you out of this land and*

lead you to the land that He promised Abraham, Isaac, and Jacob." Then, Joseph made the Hebrew people promise that when they leave Egypt they would take his body with them. When Joseph died, they embalmed his body and put it in a coffin in Egypt.

Joseph's birth is recorded in Genesis 30:22-24. Joseph was the eleventh son of Jacob. His mother was Rachel. Rachel was Laban's daughter. Laban was Rebekah's brother. Rebekah was Jacob's mother. Joseph's life story is in Genesis chapters 37-50.

Joseph was Jacob's favorite son. Perhaps, there were three reasons for this. First, Jacob loved Joseph's mother immensely. He had fallen in love with her at first sight. Second, after Jacob worked as an indentured servant for the usual seven years for the right to marry Rachel, Laban tricked him. Laban sent his eldest daughter Leah to Jacob on what would have been Rachel's wedding night. Unknowingly, Jacob slept with Leah that night.

Looking to the Future

Laban's contention was that it was customary for the elder daughter to be married before the younger. It seemed that Laban told this to Jacob a little late. So, Laban made Jacob marry Leah before he could marry Rachel. Soon after Jacob married Leah, Laban allowed Jacob to marry Rachel. However, Jacob had to serve as an indentured servant for an additional seven years to fulfill his obligation to Laban for the right to marry Rachel. Third, Jacob was about 90 years old when Joseph was born (see Principle of Belief and Practice of Faith, Seven).

When Joseph was growing up, Jacob gave him a coat of many colors. Apparently, that was special in those days. In addition, by giving Joseph such a coat, Jacob probably meant to give Joseph leadership over his older brothers. It was even possible that Jacob meant to make Joseph the head of the tribe. Undoubtedly, Joseph's brothers became jealous of him because he received the coat of many colors.

Actually, in two dreams Joseph saw that he would be superior to his brothers. Strangely, he even told his brothers about the dreams.

In the first dream, all the brothers were tying bundles of wheat. Then, all the bundles stood up. Next, the brothers' bundles gathered around Joseph's bundle. Finally, the brothers' bundles bowed down to Joseph's bundle. This appeared to have meant that Joseph would rule over his brothers.

In the second dream, Joseph saw the sun, the moon, and eleven stars bowing down to him. This dream seemed to have suggested that Joseph would be a great leader and his brothers would serve him. As you would expect, these dreams made Joseph's brothers angry with him.

When Joseph was seventeen years old, Jacob sent him to check on his brothers. They were taking care of the family's flock of animals at Shechem. When Joseph arrived in Shechem, his brothers were not there. Joseph eventually found them and the flock in Dothan. When Joseph's brothers saw him coming, they decided to kill him. It seems that their jealousy and anger turned to hate.

Looking to the Future

Did the brothers think that Joseph came to spy on them? Had Jacob used Joseph to inform on his brothers before? Were Joseph's brothers afraid that he would tell their father that they had moved the flock from Shechem to Dothan? Was this a cause for the brothers to be concerned? Whatever the answers are, it is not unheard of for parents to use favorite children as tattletales on their siblings.

One of the brothers, Reuben, persuaded the others to throw Joseph alive into a pit instead of killing him. It was Reuben's intention to rescue Joseph later. In the absence of Reuben, the brothers saw a caravan of Ishmaelites going to Egypt and sold Joseph to them. Then, they smeared the blood of a goat they had killed on Joseph's coat of many colors. They took the coat to Jacob with the story that a wild beast had killed Joseph.

In Egypt, the Ishmaelites sold Joseph as a slave to Potiphar, an official of Pharaoh. Potiphar was the captain of Pharaoh's palace guards. Pharaoh was the title given to Egyptian rulers. Pharaohs had tremendous power over the people. Therefore, pharaohs' officials were also powerful people.

Joseph proved himself extraordinarily trust-worthy and competent working for Potiphar. Potiphar realized that God made Joseph suc-cessful in his work. Consequently, Potiphar made Joseph administrator over all the of-ficial affairs of the palace guards. This made Joseph a powerful person in Pharaoh's govern-ment. God continued to be with Joseph. Thus, Joseph prospered in everything that he did. Accordingly, Potiphar's household prospered under Joseph's administration.

However, Potiphar's wife made improper ad-vances toward Joseph almost daily. Each time Joseph rejected them. Joseph did not want to sin against God or to betray Potiphar's trust. One day, Joseph went to work in the house where Potiphar wife was. Joseph was the only worker in the house at the time. Potiphar's wife grabbed Joseph and his coat came off. Joseph ran from her leaving his coat in her hands. Then, Potiphar's wife called other workers to the house and used Joseph's coat as evidence that he made improper advances toward her and left it when she screamed for help. Later, she told her husband the same story. As a result, Potiphar became angry with Joseph and put him in prison with prisoners who had committed offences against Pharaoh.

Joseph remained in prison for many years. But, God continued to be with him. Joseph was successful in all that he did in prison. Therefore, the prison administrator found Joseph trustworthy. Eventually, the prison administrator placed Joseph in charge of all the prisoners. The prison administrator also delegated other administrative responsibilities of the prison to Joseph.

Two of the prisoners who were under Joseph's charge were former officials of Pharaoh, his chief butler, and his chief cook. In time, Joseph interpreted a dream for each of them.

The chief butler told Joseph that he dreamt that he saw a vine with three branches budding and blossoming then turning to ripened grapes. The chief butler said that he was holding

Pharaoh's cup. He took the grapes and squeezed the juice out of them into Pharaoh's cup. The chief butler also said that he gave the cup to Pharaoh. Joseph told the chief butler that before the end of three days he would return to his former position in Pharaoh's palace. Joseph asked the chief butler to speak to Pharaoh about releasing him from prison. The chief butler promised to speak to Pharaoh about Joseph.

The chief baker was pleased that Joseph's explanation of the chief butler's dream was good. So, the chief baker told Joseph about his dream. The chief baker said that he dreamt there were three breadbaskets on his head. In the top basket, there were many kinds of baked goods for Pharaoh. However, birds were eating the food in the basket. Joseph told the chief baker that before the end of three days Pharaoh would make three things happen to him: His head would be cut off, his body would hang on a pole, and birds would eat his flesh.

Three days later, on Pharaoh's birthday, he gave a banquet for all his officials. On that occasion, Pharaoh freed the chief butler and the chief baker from prison. Presumably, pharaohs on their birthdays granted clemency to prisoners. Nonetheless, the chief baker was hung but the chief butler was restored to his position.

Remarkably, for two years the chief butler neglected to speak to Pharaoh concerning Joseph. Then, Pharaoh had two dreams that nobody, even his magicians and wise men, could interpret. Suddenly, the chief butler remembered Joseph. The chief butler subsequently told Pharaoh that Joseph had the gift of interpreting dreams.

Pharaoh sent for Joseph. Pharaoh told Joseph that he dreamt he stood on the edge of a river. He observed seven fat and beautiful cows emerged from the river and ate grass. Then, he saw seven thin and ugly cows come up from the river. They were the worst looking cows he ever saw in Egypt. The seven thin and ugly cows ate the seven fat and beautiful cows. After eating the fat cows, the thin cows looked the same as before. Then Pharaoh woke up.

When Pharaoh went to sleep again, he dreamt that he saw seven full-grown heads of grain on one stalk. Following that, seven heads of grain sprang up, thin and burned by the desert wind. The thin heads of grain ate the seven full-grown heads.

Joseph interpreted the dreams for Pharaoh to mean that there would be seven years of abundance of food followed by seven years of famine. Joseph suggested that the surplus food from the years of abundant produce should be stored to use during the time of famine. Consequently, Pharaoh appointed Joseph governor of all Egypt, a position of authority next to Pharaoh. Thus, Joseph executed the plans that he suggested to Pharaoh.

The famine that Joseph predicted affected the entire known world. People from many countries went to Egypt to buy grain including Joseph's brothers from Canaan. Joseph's brothers did not recognize Joseph but he knew them. Joseph cleverly accused his brothers of being spies. Joseph put his brothers in prison for three days then insisted that Simeon stay while the others bring back the youngest brother, Benjamin. Joseph and Benjamin had the same mother, Rachel.

Joseph's brothers returned with Benjamin. Joseph finally revealed himself to them. Hence, because they humbled themselves before him, the visions that he had about them bowing down to him were fulfilled. Finally, Joseph sent for his father, Jacob, and the entire family. From then on, they lived in Egypt.

• Is My Father Still Alive?

Maybe, Joseph was extremely harsh with his brothers because he was testing them to see if their characters had changed. In fact, led by Reuben, the brothers even wondered if they were being punished for the crime they committed against Joseph. In addition, they were somewhat forthright in telling Joseph that one of their brothers was missing.

Regardless, it was an extremely emotional period for Joseph even though it was obvious that he wanted to reconcile with his brothers.

Thus, there were at least three instances when Joseph experienced great emotional turmoil in dealing with his brothers. First, Joseph wept bitterly after the initial encounter with his brothers even as he did not reveal to them who he was. Second, on revealing who he was to his brothers, Joseph was overcome completely by his emotions. Third, after Jacob's death, Joseph cried profusely when he forgave his brothers for the evil they did to him.

We often experience deep unsettling feelings before we reconcile with other people. These can be stressful times because we try to contain our anger as well as to forget the past, regardless of who was wrong. Then, we are never quite certain how others will react when we reach out to them.

Apart from Joseph's yearning to see his brother Benjamin, there was another profoundly moving reason for his wanting to reconcile with his brothers. The reason was Joseph's concern for his father. First, when Joseph met his brothers he wanted to know if their father was still alive. Then, when the brothers returned with Benjamin, Joseph asked again if Jacob was still alive.

Furthermore, when Joseph was growing up, he was arrogant and boastful. Therefore, with each terrible event that Joseph experienced, God taught him humility. So, Joseph needed to reconcile with his brothers as much as they needed to reconcile with him.

Drawing from the typology of Joseph's reconciliation with his brothers, we see reasons why reconciliations are important to us. Although people might do bad things to us, sometimes we share some of the blame. Our negative actions toward other people from time to time result in bad reactions from them. If we are open to reconciliation, we will see that lots of times we need to reconcile with others as much as they need to reconcile with us.

Drawing from the passage of Scripture below, we also see reasons why reconciliations are vital to us.

All things are of God Who has reconciled us to Himself by Jesus Christ and

*has given us the ministry of reconcilia-
tion. In that, God was in Christ, reconciling the world to Him, not imputing
their sins to them, and has committed
to us the word of reconciliation. 2 Corinthians 5:18-19*

From the above passage of Scripture, we see that there are three types of reconciliations for believers. These types are reconciliation with God, reconciliation with other people, and reconciliation with ourselves.

1. Reconciliation with God

*All things are of God Who has recon-
ciled us to Himself by Jesus Christ.*

We reconcile with God through two processes. The first is confession and the second is forgiveness.

We confess our belief in Christ in order to be saved.

Looking to the Future

*If you shall **confess** with your mouth the Lord Jesus, and shall believe in your heart that God has raised Him from the dead, you shall be **saved**. Because with the heart a person believes unto righteousness and with the mouth confession is made unto salvation. Romans 10: 9-10*

Our belief in Christ's death and resurrection allows us to confess our sins to God. When we confess our sins to God He **forgives** us of our sins.

*If we confess our sins, He is faithful and just to **forgive** our sins, and to **cleanse us from all unrighteousness**. 1 John 1:9*

In summary, we are saved through Jesus Christ to be reconciled with God. For us, this is a restoration by God of the original relationship that He had with Adam. Therefore, the ultimate aim of God is for us to reconcile with

Him because without it we are alienated from Him. That is why 1 Corinthians 15:45 speaks of Jesus, "the Life Giver," as "the <u>Last</u> Adam."

2. <u>Reconciliation with other people</u>

And has given us the ministry of rec-onciliation. In that, God was in Christ, reconciling the world to Him, not im-puting their sins to them.

We reconcile with others because through Christ we have the capacity to forgive others especially if we have reconciled with God.

Confess your faults one to another and pray one for another… James 5:16

Sustained relationships between people usually need occasional reconciliations. In fact, reconciliations frequently strengthen re-lationships. Often, when people forgive each other, *lessons are learned, truths are revealed, and scars are healed.*

Looking to the Future

- o When *lessons are learned,* they often help people to avoid similar misunderstandings in the future between them and others.

- o When *truths are revealed,* they allow people to experience each other deeper.

- o When *scars are healed,* they help people to see the strengths and weaknesses that others bring to relationships due to prior bad experiences.

3. <u>Reconciliation with ourselves</u>

And has committed to us the word of reconciliation.

When we reconcile with God and other people we can be **completely honest with ourselves. We can confess (admit) our faults to ourselves and forgive ourselves for our mistakes** that affect our lives. The verse below clearly indicates a personal and reciprocal involvement in confession and forgiveness.

Principles of Belief and Practices of Faith

Confess your faults one to another...
that you may be healed. *James 5:16*

The phrase "one to another' includes **us**! We should reconcile with ourselves because it helps to enhance our self-worth. We have to see ourselves clearly, before we can evaluate or even appreciate others in our relationships with them.

> *Jesus said, "Why do you see the speck of sawdust that is in your brother's or sister's eye, but do not see the log that is in your own eye? How can you say to your brother, 'Let me remove the speck of sawdust out of your eye and a log is in your own eye?' You hypocrite, first remove the log out of your own eye then you will see clearly to remove the speck of sawdust out of your brother's or sister's eye." Matthew 7:3-5*

Ultimately, Joseph's reconciliation with his brothers, and himself, could not be complete without reuniting with his father. These typologies parallel the three types of reconciliations. The imagery here is that our *Father is alive!* That's why is necessary for us to engage in the three types of reconciliations for us to have a good relationship with God.

• Joseph as a Type of Jesus

Several characteristics about Joseph easily make him a type of Jesus. When we type Joseph to Jesus, we see the importance of looking to the future. Each type below looked to a positive outcome in the future.

Abandonment
Joseph's brothers put him in a pit (Genesis 37:20-22).
Jesus was buried in a tomb (Matthew 27:58-60).

Trustworthiness

Joseph was trustworthy in Potiphar's premises, Pharaoh's prison, and Pharaoh's palace (Genesis 39-41).

Jesus was trustworthy because He suffered and died for us (Luke 23:46).

Emotional Identity

Joseph wept before he reunited with his brothers (Genesis 43:30).

Jesus wept before he called his friend Lazarus back to life (John 11:35).

Reconciliation

Joseph reconciled with his brothers even though they tried to kill him (Genesis 45:1).

Jesus reconciled us to God while we were sinners (Luke 23:34).

• Expect Changes in the Future

Seventy people descended from Jacob when Joseph was already in Egypt. Exodus 1:5

Looking to the Future

Eventually, Joseph's family and descendants successfully settled in Egypt. The term or designation "the Hebrew people" is probably a better description ethnically at that time for Joseph's family and descendants. However, the Bible regularly refers to them as Israelites. This is generally because they were descendants of Jacob whose name was changed to Israel. Also, it might be anachronistic. That is, the name Israelites makes it easier to understand who the people were historically.

The Israelites prospered in Egypt! Yet God had promised that the Israelites would go back home! Therefore, God's intention was not for the Israelites to prosper permanently in Egypt.

In terms of the fulfillment of God's promise to the Israelites, Egypt was the in the meanwhile of their belief and faith . The promise was to be fulfilled in Canaan.

Likewise, for believers in Christ, the promise of God is fulfilled in Jesus; even if our present prosperity is not permanent. Canaan in this regard is a typology of our future everlasting dwelling place with God. Our "bodies" will be "taken" to heaven.

There is an element of belief and faith in what we expect others to engage in on our behalf after we die. In part, this is why we make wills and have people promise to do things for us after we die. In this regard, Joseph fulfilled God's promise when he instructed the people to take his embalmed body back to Canaan.

Joseph even after his death shared in the Abrahamic Promise of God! Again, this is comparable to heaven for us in that God's promise for us through Christ is completely fulfilled after we die. While we should enjoy the prosperity that Christ gives us as witnesses to the power of God on earth, we should always be mindful that each of us is on a "journey." Albeit that our journeys might be full of the "downs and ups" of the "in the meanwhiles" of our principles of beliefs and practices of faith.

Looking to the Future

As Mark 8:36-37 states:

For what shall it profit a person, if he or she shall gain the whole world and lose his or her own soul? Or, what shall a person give in exchange for his or her soul?

By what I have said about expecting changes in the future, I am not suggesting that we live focusing on death. *We don't "live to die." Indeed, we "die to live."*

• Downs and Ups in Faith Journeys

"Joseph's journey" from Canaan to Egypt and back to Canaan, is a good way to describe his "walk with God." This description is highlighted by several metaphors that I call "downs and ups."

> ➢ Joseph was thrown **down** into a pit by his brothers.

Principles of Belief and Practices of Faith

- ➢ Joseph was brought **up** from the pit by his brothers and they sold him to a caravan of Ishmaelites merchants.

- ➢ Joseph was brought **down** to Egypt by the Ishmaelites.
- ➢ Joseph was brought **up** from slavery by Potiphar.

- ➢ Joseph was brought **down** to prison because of the lies of Potiphar's wife.
- ➢ Joseph was brought **up** from prison by Pharaoh.

- ➢ Joseph's body was put **down** into a tomb in Egypt by the Egyptians.
- ➢ Joseph's body was brought **up** to Canaan by the Hebrew people.

Additionally, a metaphor of "down and up" is in God's promise to Jacob before he went to Egypt.

Israel with all his possessions went to Beersheba. There, Israel offered

334

*sacrifices to the God of his father Isaac. God spoke to Israel in visions by night. God said, "Jacob, Jacob!" Israel replied, "Here am I." God said, "I am God, the God of your father. Do not be afraid to go **down** to Egypt because there I will make you a great nation. I will go **down** with you to Egypt but also I will surely bring you **up** again. Joseph shall close your eyes. Genesis 46:1-4*

The metaphors of downs and ups connected to various facets of the Principle Belief and the Practice of Faith of "Looking to the Future" allow us to look to the future when things are going bad. When things are going bad we might be concerned and intimidated about knowing the future. We certainly don't want to know about the bad stuff that *might* be in our future. In fact, at times we don't even want to think about the future. This might explain why many people, including Christians, plan so poorly for the future. Here are examples. People are often apprehensive about taking out life insurance and making wills. They feel that these things might make bad things happen to them in the immediate future. Ironically, as people live longer, fear of bad things happening in the future become even more prevalent as they age. Living wills, healthcare proxy, and power of attorney are some of the things that numerous people are reluctant to use for living successfully. They believe that these things portend bad stuff happening to them or may even cause them to die in the near future.

In addition, the metaphors of downs and ups connected to various facets of this Principle Belief and the Practice of Faith allow us to look to the future even when things are going good. When things are going good in our lives, we sometimes get uneasy feelings. We wonder how long the good times will last. Why do we worry when we are living successfully? Instead of worrying, perhaps it would be better to ask God to show us what is in His will for us in the future. God's will for us is always about positive things happening to us in the future even though some negatives things *might* happen to us now and then. *Worrying about things going bad for us in the future diminishes belief and faith.*

The Principle of Belief and Practice of Faith of Looking to the Future in a sense is looking into the future. However, looking into the future with this Principle of Belief and Practice of Faith is not the same as looking into a crystal ball. In fact, it's not fortune-telling. Trying to predict the future using those means and others such as reading tea leaves and using tarots are methods that are full of guesses and uncertainties to say the least. On the other hand, looking into the future in terms of this principle and practice helps us make successful decisions because it involves God's promises to us. God's promises are never wrong. Therefore, this Principle of Belief and Practice of Faith is about guidance from God.

• Seeing the Future

In as much as looking to the future through the essentials of this Principle of Belief and

Practice of Faith lets us *see* the future, for this and other reasons, it is important to tell stories of belief and faith to our children and other young people.

I related in <u>Principles of Belief and Practices of Faith,</u> Looking for Miracles, Believing in the Impossible, that my maternal grandmother was blessed by an incredible miracle. Fifty-four years after my grandmother's miracle at the church, my wife and I had to make an important family decision. The decision had to do with relocating the family several thousand miles away from where we lived. In order to arrange for the relocation, I traveled by train to the same city where my mother was born. When I arrived there, I discovered that we did not have the necessary resources to accomplish what we wanted to do. So, I started to go back to the train station to return home. I had traveled by train to that city to transact business and returned home the same day many times previously. The train station was very conveniently located to walk to and from the business district of the city. For this reason, I always walked the same route to the train station from the business district. However, on that particular day, I took another route to walk to the station. In retrospect, it must have been the Spirit of God leading me.

As I started to pass by a church, a very unusual feeling came over me. First, my head felt weightless. Next, I felt like I was outside of my body. After that, it seemed as though something was preventing me from passing the church. Then it occurred to me that this was a sign that I should go back and transact our family matter of relocation. I returned to the business offices and my negotiations were successful.

For years, I wondered if the church where I had the out of body experience could have been the same church where my mother's life was spared by a miracle. After all, the church was on a hill as my grandmother said and it was close to the neighborhood where she lived at that time.

Thirty-six years after my spiritual experience at the church, I returned to that city. I always remembered my experience at the church so I went to take pictures of the area. As I was taking pictures, I experienced lightheadedness. Suddenly, I realized that each time my grandmother recounted her miraculous story to me when I was a child; I had a vision of the surrounding buildings. The buildings around the church looked the same as the buildings in my visions.

Like Joseph, many of us have the capacity through the Holy Spirit to see the future by visions and revelations. Time and again, they are related to our ancestors' prophetic experiences. We need to be more aware of these spiritual blessings.

My grandmother's miracle that blessed her with my mother was also for me. I am wrapped up in the miracle in terms of my own experiences. The decision that I made that resulted from my extraordinary experience at the church was influenced by my grandmother's spiritual experience at the same place many years before. I have had other spiritual experiences that I can easily connect to many stories of spiritual experiences of my grandmother. Many of those stories helped me in my spiritual journey to see the future.

Moreover, the spiritual gifts that my grandmother possessed, I was also blessed with. I believe that this was due partly to the fact that I paid close attention to my grandmother when she recounted the miracle at the church and many other spiritual experiences that she had. Unquestionably, I believe that I always had those spiritual gifts. God gave them to me. I also prayed for them. However, my experiences with my grandmother helped to develop and foster them.

The truth is that more believers need to grow in their understanding of spiritual gifts. Unlike many people, my grandmother had a strong and positive attitude toward prophecy, visions, and spiritual discernment. A list of these gifts is in 1 Corinthians 12:7-11.

We can see various kinds of Spiritual gifts in people. These gifts benefit all of us. Some people are given the spirit of wisdom. Others are given spiritual knowledge. Some receive a particular gift of faith. Others receive the gift of healing. Some receive the gift of working miracles. Others receive the gift of prophecy. Some are gifted to discern spirits and spiritual things. Some are gifted to speak in spiritual languages. Some receive the gift of interpreting these spiritual languages. All these gifts come from the same Spirit Who determines who receives them.

Historically, these gifts have always operated in believers. Likewise, we see many of these gifts operating in people today. Since God gives us these gifts, we should always be open-minded to the extraordinary things that these spiritual blessings are capable of accomplishing.

Certainly, my grandmother believed and practiced her spiritual gifts. Practicing these spiritual gifts helped my grandmother to be physically blessed. This is a component of living successfully. My grandmother died when she was ninety-four years old. During her lifetime, she had no major deceases or illnesses.

Overall, for this principle and practice to help us live successfully, we should always be willing to give credence to the incomprehensible things in life. We should not attribute extraordinary events just to incidents and coincidences or permutations and probabilities. Since the inexplicable things in life are not necessarily accidents, God wants us to see certain aspects of the future that pertain to us.

> Paul said, "Although there is nothing to gain from you by it, I will go on bragging. Let me tell you about visions and revelations of the Lord. I know a man in Christ who about fourteen years ago (whether in the body, I cannot tell; or whether out of the body, I cannot tell. Only God knows) was brought up to the third heaven. I knew such a man (whether in the body or out of the body, I cannot tell. Only God knows).

He was brought up to paradise and heard things that are not explainable and that he is not allowed to tell."
2 Corinthians 12:1-4

Clearly, the "out of the body" experience of Paul allowed him see into the future through "visions and revelations." Visions and revelations both frequently relate to the future. This is evident in Joseph's gift of interpreting dreams.

• Looking to the Future

The legacy of going back home to be buried in Canaan to fulfill prophecy is not attributed to Joseph alone. Jacob requested to be buried in Canaan before Joseph did.

Joseph embraced his father, wept on him, and kissed him. Joseph commanded his servants, the physicians, to embalm his father. The embalming process took the usual forty days.

Looking to the Future

After that, the Egyptians mourned for him for thirty days. When the days of his mourning were past, Joseph spoke to Pharaoh's palace officials. Joseph said, "If now I have found favor with you, please speak to Pharaoh. Tell him that my father made me take an oath. He said, 'I will soon die. In the burial place that I hewed out for myself in the land of Canaan, there you shall bury me' Now therefore, I plea with you, let me go up, bury my father, and I will return." Consequently, Pharaoh told Joseph, "Go up, and bury your father according to how he made you promise." Genesis 50:1-6

The above promise that Joseph fulfilled was a continuation of the promise that God made to Abraham. God had promised Abraham several times that his descendants would dwell in Canaan. Two of these occasions are stated below.

Principles of Belief and Practices of Faith

In Genesis 13:14-17, God made the promise to Abraham that his descendants would be many and they would possess much land. Specifically, God said to Abraham:

> "Lift up now your eyes. Look from where you are, northward, southward, eastward, and westward because all the land that you see, I will give to you and your descendants forever. I will make your descendants as the dust of the earth, so that if a person could number the dust of the earth, then, your descendants could be numbered. Arise; walk through the land in the length and breadth of it because I will give it to you."

Again, in Genesis 15:18 God made a covenant (contract or treaty) with Abraham that his descendants would occupy an extensive area of land. Specifically, God said to Abraham:

Looking to the Future

"I give this land to your progeny, from the river of Egypt to the great river Euphrates."

Therefore, the legacy of Jacob's burial in Canaan was in a sense part of the fulfillment of the Abrahamic promise. When I say legacy I mean that the root of securing a burial place for Jacob was established in the promise that God made to Abraham that the Israelites would inherit land in Canaan.

Jacob's sons carried him into the land of Canaan and buried him in the cave of the field of Machpelah, near Mamre. ***Abraham had bought the field for a burial place from Ephron the Hittite.*** *Genesis 50:13*

The burial place in Canaan is also symbolic of the continued presence of the Israelites in the Promised Land.

Principles of Belief and Practices of Faith

Interestingly, Moses was also a part of the legacy of God's promise to Abraham for two reasons:

1) Joseph's burial in Canaan represented a continued dwelling of the descendants of Abraham in that land.
2) Joseph's burial in Canaan fulfilled a promise that pointed to the *future blessings of the Hebrew people.*

> *Moses took the bones of Joseph with him because he had made the sons of Israel swore an oath saying, "God will surely come to your rescue and you shall carry up my bones from here with you." Exodus 13:19*

Sometimes for us to see the future, we have to look to the future because *the past was the future.* Certainly, events are always clearer in hindsight. *The present was also the future.* We definitely think that we have some control of the present. Yet, the challenge for us is to see the future as we see events retrospectively and currently.

The following events involving Shechem underscore how looking to the future can make us see the future. These events pointed to Shechem as a place of inheritance for the Hebrew people.

- ***Shechem was the place mentioned when Abraham first arrived in Canaan*** (Genesis 12:6).
- ***It was in Shechem that God first made the promise to Abraham that his descendants would inherit the land*** (Genesis 12:7).
- ***Abraham built his first altar to God at Shechem*** (Genesis 12:7).
- ***Jacob sent Joseph to Shechem to check on his brothers. That event led to Joseph being sold as a slave in Egypt*** (Genesis 37:12-14).
- ***A parcel of land that Jacob bought in Shechem became Joseph's burial place*** (Genesis 33:18-19).

The bones of Joseph that the children of Israel brought up from Egypt, they buried in Shechem, in a parcel of land that Jacob bought from the sons of Hamor the father of Shechem for a hundred pieces of silver. **The plot of land became the inheritance of the children of Joseph.** *Joshua 24:32*

Prophecies that are tied to God's promises are meant for successful living in the future. This is true even if in the meanwhile people might try to do us harm. In fact, what they mean for evil will result in good things happening to us and our descendants. The passage below speaks loudly of this.

After Joseph buried his father, he returned to Egypt with his brothers and all the people who went up with them. When Joseph's brothers realized the possible consequences of their father's death they said, "Joseph probably still hates us. He will certainly repay us for

all the evil that we did to him." Then, the brothers sent a messenger to Joseph. The messenger said, "Your father commanded us before he died to say to you, 'Forgive us for the harm, sin, and evil that we did to you. Forgive the crime of the servants of the God of your father.'" Joseph wept as they spoke to him. His brothers bowed down to him and said, "We will be your slaves." Joseph said to them, "Be not afraid. I do not take the place of God. You planned evil against me but God meant it for good, to bring to pass as it is this day, to save many people lives."
Genesis 50:14-20

We have to believe in the future because after death we have no control over earthly matters. Actually, the reality of life is the reality of faith. If things in our lives get bad then they can get better, notwithstanding the Christian perspective of death. That is, believers know that we go to a better place and life after we die. However, our faith would be limited un-less we believe that things will get better here if they should get bad. We just can't resign our-selves to wait until we get to heaven for things to get better. We need to believe in the future so that we might *act in faith in the present.*

> *As it is written, "Eye has not seen, nor ear heard, neither have entered into the heart of people, the things that God has prepared for them who love Him." 1 Corinthians 2:9*

What might be some experiences that you are having right now that may affect those people who come after you? The way you be-lieve and the way you act in faith regarding these things will help to determine whether you live successfully!

PRINCIPLE AND PRACTICE TEN
Overcoming Fear

By faith Moses, when he was born his parents hid him for three months because they saw that he was an unusual child and they were not afraid of Pharaoh's ruling. Hebrews 11: 23

- ## Growth through Faith

In due course, Joseph, all his brothers, and everyone of that generation died. As time went on, the population of the children of Israel increased tremendously so that the land was filled with them. <u>Then, a new Pharaoh, who did not know who Joseph was, came to power in Egypt.</u> Pharaoh said to his people, "Look, the people of the *children of Israel are more and mightier than we are. Come on; let us deal wisely with them before they become larger and if there should be war they join with our enemies to fight against us. So, rid them from the land." Therefore, the Egyptians placed over the Israelites, taskmasters to afflict them with burdens. They built for Pharaoh the treasure cities of Pithom and Raamses. But, the more the Egyptians afflicted the Israelites, the more they multiplied and grew. The Egyptians became frustrated with the children of Israel. Exodus 1:6-12*

I generally conclude that when Joseph was an administrator in Egypt, the pharaohs were perhaps culturally and ethnically closer to the Hebrew people than previous Egyptian rulers were. The pharaohs in the time of Joseph could have been Hyksos. The Hyksos were from Canaan. Because of their own experiences as shepherds, they would have empathized with the nomadic and pastoral Hebrew people. Actually, the Egyptian word Hyksos, sometimes translated "shepherd kings," most likely meant "nomadic foreign rulers." Following this trend of thought, the Pharaoh who favored Joseph, his family, and the Hebrew people was probably Apopi (or Apopis). When the Hebrew people arrived in Egypt, Apopi gave them an area of land called Goshen. Goshen probably meant "the best of the land."

When the rule of the Hyksos ended, the descendants of Jacob were allowed to live in Goshen undisturbed with their possessions, but after the death of Joseph, the Egyptians became suspicious of the Hebrew people and eventually came to hate them. The fact that the Hebrew people lived in a choice Egyptian territory certainly didn't help their relations with the Egyptians. Then, "a new Pharaoh" started to rule who was not familiar with the legacy of Joseph. In consequence, the period of slavery of the Hebrew people began.

• **Faith Growth not People Swelling**

Central to the retelling of the long history of the children of Israel as slaves in Egypt is that their numbers kept increasing in spite of their hardships and the attempts by the Egyptian authorities to inflict genocide on them. Pharaoh's intention was genocide since he ordered all the Hebrew male babies killed. Certainly, this plan would have destroyed the Hebrew people as an ethnic group.

Pharaoh's goal to kill all the male Hebrew babies is a *typology of real life.* The evil that exits in the world is intent on destroying our abilities to live successfully. Ultimately, should this be accomplished we would be destroyed. However, God's plan is for us to live successfully and not to be destroyed.

> *Pharaoh spoke to the Hebrew mid-wives Shiphrah and Puah. He said, "When you work as midwives to the*

Overcoming Fear

Hebrew women and see them giving birth to babies on the delivery stools; if the baby is a boy, then you shall kill him, but if the baby is a girl, then she shall live." Nevertheless, the midwives feared God and did not do as Pharaoh commanded them. They saved the male children. Then Pharaoh called for the midwives and said to them, "Why have you saved the male children?" The midwives told Pharaoh, "Because the Hebrew women are not as the Egyptian women. They are strong and they give birth to their babies before the midwives come to them." Exodus 1:15-19

While the text above might suggest that the midwives were making excuses to Pharaoh why they did not follow his orders, there might have been other things occurring.

First, the midwives feared God, *not Pharaoh!* Actually, it appears that the midwives feared God for several reasons. The midwives names are not Egyptian, their names are Semitic, most likely Ugaritic (Canaanite). They were in all probability Hebrew women. It is not conceivable that Egyptian women served Hebrew women as midwives. These things suggest that the midwives had some relationships with the Hebrew people. Moreover, since the midwives feared Yahweh, some Hebrew people probably had some knowledge of the same God. He would have been their God!

Second, the Hebrew women indeed were likely stronger than Egyptian women as a whole. Physical labor might have made the Hebrew women more robust as opposed to the comparative inactive life of some Egyptian women - especially the privileged class of women. The Hebrew women's health could have been a reason why their numbers kept increasing under the difficult conditions of bondage. Pharaoh would not have known these things necessarily.

The midwives trusted in God because they knew about the Hebrew women's health and they were certain that Pharaoh would accept their report. Thus, we can make the connection that the midwives did not fear Pharaoh because of their *belief* and *faith* in God according to Hebrews 11:6 and the Principle of Belief and Practice of Faith of Overcoming Fear.

An element of faith through belief relates to how we grow spiritually. I propose that perhaps another reason why the Hebrew people increased in numbers was that they were prospering spiritually through the legacies of their ancestors. Whether the Hebrew people knew it or not, Egypt was not their final home. The journey into slavery was not their final stop. Their freedom from bondage was implied every time God promised Abraham, Isaac, and Jacob that their descendants would inherit territories in Canaan.

Sometimes, we grow stronger in faith because of adversity. However, *spiritual growth is not simply a result of surviving hardship. We grow spiritually without hardship also!* Yet, spiritual growth under difficult circumstances usually indicates that we have achieved a wealth of spiritual strength. *It is difficult to survive*

extreme hardship without deep belief and enduring faith.

According to Paul,

> "Therefore, I am content in my weak-
> nesses; whenever I am insulted, during
> hard times, in my sufferings, when I ex-
> perience all sorts of trouble for Christ's
> sake, because when I am weak, then
> am I strong." 2 Corinthians 12:10

Essential to the understanding of faith
growth is experiencing what I call "miracles of
spiritual multiplications." I use this term based
on being inspired by a statement in a disser-
tation by Dr. Gloria Elena Adams. Dr. Adams
wrote that once when she was on a street with
her Dramatic Resource Ministry, the group ren-
dered a dramatic reading of Luke 9:12-17. The
reading was about how Jesus miraculously
multiplied a small amount of fish and bread
and fed thousands of people. After the reading, someone in the crowd shouted that the
community needed a "food multiplier." This re-

mark was related to the government's cutbacks on food stamps and other food programs for those in need of those services. It struck me that the term food multiplier could be applied to many spiritual situations.

In my view, the Bible recorded several miracles of spiritual multiplications. For the purpose of this principle and practice, I chose two instances from the writings of Mark.

The first instance is in Mark 6:30-44. After a busy schedule of preaching by Jesus' disciples, they gathered around Him to report what they had experienced. As they met, crowds of people kept coming to them. Jesus and His followers had no time to eat and rest. Jesus suggested that they retire to a quiet place. So, they headed for an isolated area to get into a boat. However, many people saw them leaving. The news spread to many surrounding towns telling people where Jesus and His disciples were going. A great amount of people ran to the place where Jesus and His disciples were going and arrived there before them.

Principles of Belief and Practices of Faith

When Jesus arrived and saw the large crowd, he had compassion on them because they seemed to be wandering without direction and leadership. Jesus taught the multitude many things. When it became late in the day, the disciples urged Jesus to send the crowd away so that they could purchase food in the surrounding towns. Jesus' reply was that the disciples should feed the crowd. The disciples answered that they certainly did not have enough money to buy food to feed the multitude. It was then that Jesus proceeded to have His disciples feed the people. They fed over five thousand people with five loaves of bread and two fish.

The second instance is in Mark 8:1-9. This time, after a large throng of people followed Jesus for three days, He remarked to His disciples that the people had nothing to eat. Jesus was concerned about sending the crowd home hungry and some people becoming ill. Again, the disciples thought that feeding such a large crowd with little resources was impossible. Once more, Jesus made his disciples feed the mass. They fed over four thousand people with seven loaves of bread and a few small fish.

These miracles of multiplications can be exponential. In the first miracle, twelve baskets were filled with bread and fish that remained after the people ate. In the second miracle, seven baskets were filled with bread and fish that remained after the people were fed. I conjecture that the bread and the fish that remained were not simply leftovers. Rather, they were portions of food that were not served. The people probably ate the portions later. This might explain why in Mark 8:14, the disciples still had *a loaf* of bread soon after the feeding of over four thousand people Furthermore, Jesus reminded them of the quantities of bread remaining after the miracles.

Now the disciples had <u>forgotten to take bread</u>, neither had they in the ship with them more than one loaf. *Jesus charged them, "Observe! Be careful of the yeast of the Pharisees* *and of the yeast of Herod." The disciples argued among themselves saying, "It is because we have no bread." Jesus knew what they were saying so He asked them, "Why are you discussing that you have no bread? Do you not perceive, or understand yet? Are your minds shut? Having eyes, do you not see? Having ears, do you not hear? Do you remember when I distributed the five loaves among five thousand people how many baskets full of remains you took up?" They replied, "Twelve." Jesus continued questioning them, "And when the seven loaves fed four thousand how many baskets full of remains did you take up?" They answered, "Seven." Then Jesus asked them, "How is it then that you do not understand?" Mark 8:14-21*

We should not focus on material growth without the benefit of spiritual growth. It is evident that Jesus taught the crowd before he performed those miracles of multiplications. It is clear also that the disciples did not see the connection between Jesus' teachings to the miracles of food multiplication. It is also obvious that there is a metaphor here that when the word of God is being spread spiritual growth is multiplying.

However, growth is not always indicative of spiritual soundness. Sometimes growth is merely "swelling." Swelling is symptomatic of disease and sickness. Believers often link success in programs and activities to numbers. We often become upset when responses to our activities are meager and attendances to our activities are small.

The crowds grew that followed Jesus because He fed them messages that they were spiritually hungry to hear, so much so that they forgot to eat physically. Then, when the crowd grew hungry for physical food, the spiritual blessings from Jesus' teaching created an environment for the multiplication of material things.

I am not suggesting necessarily that people should be taught before they are physically fed. Indeed, often people physical needs are urgent. All the same, whenever feasible we should make every attempt to nourish people spiritually as well as physically.

Christian communities and churches need to grow healthily through sound Christian teachings. That's why Jesus tells us to be aware of the yeast of insincere people. Insincere people create environments for growth without spiritual multiplication. Also, it is why many Christian organizations and churches swell but don't grow spiritually.

• **Faith Through the Bad and the Good**

The Bad

It is obvious that Pharaoh tried to use more than two Hebrew midwives to kill Hebrew baby boys because the population was growing, so to speak, exponentially. Besides this, the text below indicates or at least implies five intriguing factors about the midwives that challenged Pharaoh.

> *Therefore, God was good to the midwives and the people multiplied and became even more populous. Because the midwives feared God, he gave them families as blessings. Exodus 1:20-21*

- ❑ The first factor is that the text says, "God was good to the midwives." This indicates that Pharaoh had reasons to respect the midwives' judgment. There is no indication that Pharaoh challenged the midwives' decision.

- ❑ The second factor is that the specific names of Shiphrah and Puah are not mentioned in this text as they are in Exodus 1:15. Even so, both scriptures suggest to me that since there was a large population of Hebrew women,

Pharaoh was dealing with a large number of midwives

❑ The third factor is that, in any case, the names of the midwives stated in Exodus 1:15 may have been eponyms. That is, each name probably represented a large group of midwives.

❑ The fourth factor is that the text could be speaking about many other groups of midwives in addition to the groups of Shiphrah and Puah.

❑ The fifth factor is that the word midwives in the text is contextually parallel to the multiplication of the people's growth.

Furthermore, historically trade and professional people usually formed guilds. Those guilds were akin to today's unions. There were certainly guilds in ancient Egypt. The guilds often formed federations with other types of associations of workers. Those federations had similarities to today's federations of unions.

It is reasonable to assume that the midwives belonged to guilds at that time. Since Shiphrah and Puah were most likely eponyms for guilds, they were probably part of an association of workers. That type of federation would have made their groups stronger. In fact, that was the purpose of such federations.

Actually, the Hebrew word for family in the text is not always used literally. Frequently the word is used figuratively. Here are two examples of the figurative use of the word family. Family (house or household) can be a place where people congregate. Regularly, the word family means an extended family or a clan. Thus, the word "families" in Exodus 1:21 could imply that God blessed the midwives by strengthening their guilds and federations.

The word family might infer also, why Pharaoh had to resort to other means to kill the Hebrew boy babies. Since the midwives were powerful groups of women, Pharaoh made it the responsibility of all the people do the horrible tasks.

> *Pharaoh charged all his people by saying, "Every son who is born to the Hebrew people you shall throw into the river, but every daughter born to the Hebrew people you shall spare their lives." Exodus 1:22*

Sometimes when evil doesn't get its way, it makes the people who are doing wrong things become meaner. Pharaoh certainly did. I am sure that the midwives expected Pharaoh to become meaner. Pharaohs could be ruthless since many were revered as gods.

The midwives' belief and faith made them more successful in life. They believed that God would protect them against Pharaoh's power and they acted in faith by disobeying him.

As believers, we are strong as a people, particularly when we act together in one accord. Although evil often appears strong, we should believe in our powers through God and act in faith against what is wrong.

The Good

While Pharaoh was having Hebrew baby boys killed, a special Hebrew boy was born. We could say that in a bad situation a good situation developed. Indeed, the Middle English word in the King James Version of the Bible for the word "unusual" in the text below is "goodly."

> There was a man of the tribe of Levi who married a woman of the same tribe. The woman gave birth to a son. When she saw that he was an unusual child, she hid him for three months. Exodus 2:1-2

The first thing we should take note of is that these parents were risking their lives. Exodus 1:22 should be interpreted to mean that Pharaoh's edict included Hebrew parents and Hebrew people. Hence, these parents were not just hiding the baby from the Egyptians alone, but also they were required by Pharaoh to kill their own child. The passage below supports this extrapolation.

> *Another Pharaoh arose who did not know who Joseph was. Pharaoh dealt cleverly with our ancestors. He also was evil to our ancestors, and made them throw out their young children so that they would die. Acts 7:18-19*

We see this type of edict historically from despotic leaders. Often, these state endorsed tyrannical killings of people are connected to ethnic cleansing.

The second thing we should take note of is that this special child's parents were from the tribe of Levites. The Levites were priests. The baby boy's father Amram and mother Jochebed, were of the particular group of Levites known as the Kohathites.

One of the primary duties of the Kohathites was taking care of the Ark of the Covenant. The Ark of the Covenant was a chest. The tablets of the Ten Commandments were kept in the Ark of the Covenant. The Middle English of the King James Version of the Bible used the word "ark" for the word "basket" in the passage of Scripture below.

Incidentally, the same Hebrew word for ark used for basket in the passage below was used in Genesis 50:26 for Joseph's coffin. A function of the Ark of the Covenant was for the Levites to carry it in front of the people in their wilderness travels "to search out a resting place for them" (Numbers 10:33). Hence, Joseph's coffin being taken back to Canaan was a foreshadowing of Moses leading the people to the Promised Land with the Ark of the Covenant going before them. Later, the Ark of the Covenant, carried by the Levites, led the people of Israel over the Jordan River on dry ground into the Promised Land (see Joshua 3:1-4).

• **Trusting in God puts us on top**

*When the woman who was of the tribe of Levi could no longer hide her baby son, she made an ark (**basket**) of reeds for* *him, covered it with tar, and put the child in it. Then, she laid it in the high grassy area of the banks of the river. The baby's sister stood at a distance, observing what was being done to him. The daughter of Pharaoh came down to wash herself at the river. While Pharaoh's daughter and her servants walked along the river's side, she saw the basket among the tall grass. She sent a maid to get it. When Pharaoh's daughter opened it, she saw the child. The baby cried. She had compassion on him and said, "This is one of the Hebrews' children." Then the baby's sister asked Pharaoh's daughter, "Shall I go and call a nurse of the Hebrew women that she may nurse the child for you?" Pharaoh's daughter said to her, "Go!" The girl went and called the child's mother. Pharaoh's daughter instructed her, "Take this child away, nurse it for me, and I will pay your wages." The woman took the child and nursed it. The child grew. Eventually, the child's mother brought him to Pharaoh's daughter and he became her son. Pharaoh's daughter named the child Moses. She said, "Because I drew him out of the water." Exodus 2:3-10*

It was very likely that the river where this special Hebrew baby boy was put on in a basket was one of the areas where Hebrew baby boys had been thrown in to drown. They would most likely have sunk to the bottom of the river. In contrast, Moses was put in the basket to float on the river. In a way, we can say that God wants us to be on top. We must believe that God will always keep us afloat and away from danger in difficult circumstances.

An "in the meanwhile of faith" moment was when Moses' sister waited after she placed him in the basket on the river not knowing what would happen. I think she believed that something positive would happen. That's why she acted in faith by putting Moses securely in the river in the first place.

Nonetheless, Moses' sister was the one who offered to get a Hebrew woman to nurse the child.

The in the meanwhile of faith is not about co-incidences. The in the meanwhile of faith is about *opportunities for blessings.* There is no indication that Moses' sister expected that God would make Moses' own mother nurse him. However, when the opportunity came to Moses' sister, *she seized the moment of faith.* She arranged for Moses' mother to nurse him so that she could nurture him. Evidently, Pharaoh's daughter did not know that the Hebrew woman who nursed the child was the child's mother.

The time that Moses' mother spent nursing him was formative. This shaped Moses' future. It may have helped him to identify with the Hebrew people as he grew. Maybe in those first months, even though Moses would not have understood in the capacity that an adult would, she told him stories of his heritage. This is another reason I believe that telling children stories of faith can greatly influence their lives. This type of nurturing helps children realize later their purposes in life. The earlier we tell children stories of faith the better will be their prospects for living successfully.

PRINCIPLE AND PRACTICE ELEVEN
Making Tough Choices

By faith Moses, when he became an adult, refused to be called the son of Pharaoh's daughter, choosing to suffer affliction with the people of God than to enjoy the temporary pleasures of sin. He regarded the suffering of Christ greater riches than the treasures in Egypt because he was looking to the future for his reward. Hebrews 11:24-26

Exodus 2:11-15 record that when Moses was grown he visited the Hebrew people where they worked as slaves. There Moses saw an Egyptian man assaulting a Hebrew man. Moses checked to see if anyone was looking then he killed the Egyptian and hid the body in the sand.

When Moses returned the next day, he saw two Hebrew men fighting each other. Moses asked the man who was in the wrong, "Why are you beating a fellow Hebrew?" The Hebrew answered by wanting to know who made Moses ruler over them. Evidently, they knew that Moses was Hebrew. Then, the Hebrew asked Moses if he would kill him as he killed the Egyptian the previous day. At that moment, Moses realized that at least the incident was known among the Hebrew people. When Pharaoh heard about the murder, Moses ran away to the territory of Midian.

• Tough Choices

In Hebrews 11:24-26, I see three elements of tough choices as they relate to belief and faith.

1. <u>Tough choices often hurt.</u>

By faith Moses, when he became an adult, refused to be called the son of Pharaoh's daughter. Hebrews 11:24

Making Tough Choices

By choosing to identify with the Hebrew people, Moses undoubtedly hurt himself, Pharaoh's daughter, Pharaoh, his friends, and other people. Tough choices are not always about popularity. Trying not to hurt anyone is important for believers. Nonetheless, there are times when we have to make tough choices that may hurt people. The truth is, tough choices often hurt.

On the contrary, making easy choices can lead to greater hurt than making tough choices. For instance, frequently we have to make tough choices as to whether or not to confront people with truths regarding their negative behaviors. Invariably, they are hurt when we confront them. Yet, people often get over their hurts within reasonable periods when confronted in love with truths. On the other hand, sometimes when we don't tell people about their faults, should they be hurt by their shortcomings, only to discover that we could have helped them by telling them the truth, they are likely to be deeply wounded.

People frequently make easy choices because they want to fit in with other people. However, we should not "go along" just "to get along." When we respond by going along just to get along, we might be succumbing to "peer pressure." Although, regularly we attribute peer pressure only to young people, it is a reality for most people. Peer pressures occur at our jobs, schools, home, places of worship, and just about everywhere else that we interact with people.

Why make tough choices when they hurt? We make tough choices even though they may hurt because *only by faith we should make tough choices.*

2. <u>Tough choices can be messy</u>.

Choosing to suffer affliction with the people of God than to enjoy the temporary pleasures of sin. Hebrews 11:25

Making tough choices might create difficult situations for us. These difficulties could come from people opposing us and making our lives miserable. For instance, people might oppose us when we support things that are fair and correct. On the other hand, we generally want to please as many people as we can so commonly we don't support unpopular causes. Moreover, we tend to want to avoid messy situations in our relationships with others. However, if we don't take positions for righteous causes our inactions could be tantamount to "sinning."

3. <u>Tough choices sometimes call for personal sacrifices.</u>

   He regarded the suffering of Christ greater riches than the treasures in Egypt because he was looking to the future for his reward. Hebrews 11:26

Frequently, a common thread is evident when we make tough choices. It is how we see ourselves in the present in relation to the future. This is a struggle between reasoning, and belief and faith.

- *Reasoning* tells us not to make sacrifices and never to give up anything.
- ✓ *Belief* tells us we should give up the things that are bad for us.
- ✓ *Faith* allows us to give up things that we don't want to let go of.

- *Reasoning* tells us that we don't know what is going to happen in the future.
- ✓ *Belief* tells us that we don't have to know what will happen in the future in order to have faith.
- ✓ *Faith* makes the future we hope for a reality.

- *Reasoning* tells us to get all that we can now.
- ✓ *Belief* tells us to trust the future.
- ✓ *Faith* makes us prepare for the future.

Making Tough Choices

Finally, reasoning not only makes us struggle with what we may lose when we make tough choices, it also makes us struggle with what may replace what we give up. For instance, when people profit from doing bad things, they find it difficult to stop doing them. So, doing good things strikes them as less rewarding than doing bad things.

- Therefore, *reasoning* tells us to have as much good times now as possible.
- ✓ However, *belief* tells us "we haven't seen anything yet."
- ✓ In addition, *faith* tells us to "keep on keeping on."

Moses voluntarily chose to identify with the Hebrew people. At that time, to be a free Egyptian was an extraordinary privilege. Moses was more than a free member of the Egyptian society; he was a prince. Could Moses have become a pharaoh? *When Moses made the tough choice of siding with the Hebrews, he eliminated the possibility of him becoming a pharaoh and thereby becoming the chief oppressor of his people!*

Also, when Moses made the tough choice of siding with the Hebrews, he risked all that he acquired and was entitled to as a prince. There was the danger of going from a prince to becoming somewhat of a pauper. Most people would want to go from a pauper to a prince or princess.

Ironically, after Moses killed the Egyptian because he was beating a Hebrew man it was another Hebrew man who wanted to know from Moses who made him a ruler and judge over the Hebrew people. Actually, Moses was a prince and judge! Paradoxically, his own people rejected him!

The reality was that if Moses had continued to be a prince without fulfilling his God given purpose in life, in a sense he would have been a pauper. In fulfilling God's plan for his life, Moses really became a prince of his people in the eyes of God. Similarly, when we become what God wants us to be, we also become richly blessed. In the final analysis, we gain more than we lose when we make tough choices that are in the will of God. This helps us to live successfully.

• **Tough Choices and Typology**

There are numerous ways that the author of the book of Hebrews used typology that we can employ to underscore the importance of making tough choices relating to this principle and practice.

1. Foremost, the writer of Hebrews definitely typed Moses to Christ in Hebrews 11:26.

Moses regarded the suffering of Christ greater riches than the treasures in Egypt because he was looking to the future for his reward.

Moses
Moses chose to give up power and prestige.
Moses chose to go from riches to "rags."

Christ
Christ chose to give up power and prestige. Christ chose to go from riches to "rags."

2. Then, there are several other ways to type Moses to Jesus based the images of the eleventh chapter of Hebrews.

Moses
- ○ The original roots of the English name "Moses" in the Coptic and Hebrew languages mean, "drawn" or "drawn out" or "saved."
- ○ Moses was "saved" by his parents when they hid him for three months from the people.
- ○ Moses was "drawn out" or "saved" from the water because of Pharaoh's daughter.
- ○ Moses was "saved" when he ran away to the territory of Midian.
- ○ Moses left Midian when it was "safe" after Pharaoh died.

- o Moses became a "drawer" and "savior" of his people when he led them out of slavery to the Promised Land.

Jesus

- o The original root of the word "Jesus" in the Hebrew language is related to the word "save."
- o Jesus was "saved" when He was an infant because the wise men did not report His whereabouts to Herod the Great.
- o Jesus was "saved" when He was a child because His parents protected Him from being killed by the authorities of Herod the Great.
- o Jesus' parents took Him to Egypt to "save" His life.
- o Jesus was brought back to Palestine when it was "safe" after Herod the Great died.
- o Jesus is our "drawer" and "savior" who leads us to the Father in heaven.

3. Finally, I'm moved and amazed by how the writer in the eleventh chapter of Hebrews interpreted various aspects of the second chapter of Exodus that we can relate to the New Testament. The writer, of course, used many typologies. These interpretations as typologies *foreshadow* **Moses** to **Jesus** and *shadow* **Jesus** to **us**.

I. **Moses** was instrumental in **relieving** the Hebrew people of the **burdens** of slavery.

   a) It came to pass in those days, when Moses was grown he went to his people and saw their burdens. Moses saw an Egyptian beating a Hebrew man; one of his brothers. Exodus 2:11

II. **Jesus relieved** us of the **burdens** of sin.

   b) Come to Me all those who are tired and are overloaded and I will give you rest. Take My yoke on you, and learn from Me because I am meek and lowly in heart and you shall find rest for your souls. My yoke is easy and My burden is light! Matthew 11:28-30

III. We are to **relieve** each other of **burdens**.

c) Bear one another's burdens and so fulfill the law of Christ. Galatians 6:2

IV. Moses brought **good news** from God to the Israelites for the **world**.

d) Moses said to God, "Look, when I go to the Israelites and tell them, 'The God of your fathers sent me to you, and they ask me, what is His name?' What shall I say to them?" God said to Moses, "I AM THAT I AM." God also said, "Thus shall you say to the children of Israel, I AM has sent me to you." Moreover God told Moses, "Thus shall you say to the children of Israel, the Lord God of your fathers, the God of Abraham, Isaac, and Jacob, has sent me to you. This is My name forever and this is how I will be remembered for all generations. Exodus 3:13-15

V. Jesus brought **good news** to the **world** with His birth.

e) This shall be a sign to you, "You shall find the baby wrapped in swaddling clothes, lying in a manger." Suddenly there was with the angel a multitude of the heavenly crowd praising God saying, "Glory to God in the highest, and on earth peace, good will toward people." Luke 2:12-14

VI. We are to spread the **Good News** of Jesus throughout the **world**.

f) Jesus came and spoke to His disciples saying, "All power is given to me in heaven and on earth. Go therefore and teach all nations, baptizing them in the name of the Father, and of the Son, and of the Holy Ghost. Teach them to follow everything that I taught you. I am always with you, even to the end of the world. Amen." Matthew 28:18-20

VII. Moses' authority to do ministry was challenged.

g) The man answered Moses, "Who made you a prince and a judge over us? Do you intend to kill me as you killed the Egyptian?" Then Moses became afraid and said, "Certainly, this thing is known." Exodus 2:14

VIII. Jesus' authority to do ministry was challenged.

h) It happened that on one of those days, as Jesus taught the people in the temple and preached the gospel; the chief priests and the scribes came to Him with the elders. They said to Him, "Tell us; by what authority do You do these things? Or, who gave You this authority?" Luke 20:1-2

IX. We are **challenged** concerning our **authority** to do **ministry** as the priesthood of believers in Christ.

i) Annas the high priest, Caiaphas, John, Alexander and many who were related to the high priest gathered in Jerusalem. When they placed Peter and John in the middle of the gathering, they asked, "By what authority or by what name have you done this?" Then, Peter filled with the Holy Ghost said to them, "You rulers of the people and elders of Israel, if we today are examined for the good deed done to the crippled man and by what means he is made whole; be it known to you and all the people of Israel that it was done in the name of Jesus Christ of Nazareth. You crucified Jesus but God raised Him from the dead. Because of Jesus, this man stands here before you whole." Acts 4:6-10

• **Tough Decisions**

Making *tough choices* often means making *tough decisions*. Making tough decisions frequently means taking sides. For instance, when Moses killed the Egyptian, he later realized that more than likely other Hebrew slaves saw the slaying. Moses had made the *tough choice* of trying to help his people by slaying the Egyptian. Then he had to make the *tough decision* to flee Egypt.

Sometimes, tough decisions are associated with sin. Simply put, people often make decisions about whether they should sin or not. For example, according to Hebrews 11:25, Moses chose to suffer with his people. This resulted in his tough decision not to "sin" by undertaking his social justice responsibilities.

Similarly, elaborating on what I previously stated, we sin when there are social justice needs that we can help with but ignore them. For instance, believers should not ignore the oppression of people. People are being oppressed all over the world even in places where we are spreading the gospel of Jesus Christ. We should not spread the gospel and ignore people's oppressed conditions.

There is no question in my mind that part of the gospel is a social message. In fact, part of Jesus' ministry concerned social justice issues. He personalized social justice as our ministry to Him. Jesus said:

> *"Then shall He say also to them on the left hand, 'Depart from Me, you are condemned to the everlasting fire that is prepared for the devil and his angels. I was hungry and you gave Me no food. I was thirsty and you gave Me no drink. I was a stranger and you*

did not take Me in. I was naked and you did not clothe Me. I was sick and you did not visit Me. I was in prison and you did not visit Me.' Then they also shall answer Him, 'Lord, when did we see You hungry, or thirsty, or a stranger, or naked, or sick, or in prison, and did not minister to You?' Then He shall answer them, 'Honestly, I say to you, as much as you did not do it to one of the least of these people, you did not do it to Me.'" Matthew 25:41-45

Since believers have social justice responsibilities then overall the church has social responsibilities to everyone who is in need. However, many churches have not made the tough decisions to create social programs for their communities. They see these programs as contrary to their religious and spiritual obligations. Could it be that these are easy choices for them in comparison to the tough choices and tough decisions of the "followship" of Jesus?

PRINCIPLE AND PRACTICE TWELVE
Waiting

By faith Moses left Egypt, not fearing the anger of Pharaoh. He endured as though he saw the Person Who is invisible. Hebrews 11: 27

It is interesting that the writer of the Book of Hebrews did not interpret Moses' running away from Egypt to Midian as being afraid that Pharaoh would kill him. The writer said that Moses fled because it was as if he saw the invisible God with him.

Indeed, the Scripture teaches us that God's power is often around us in mighty ways whether we see it or not. This is illustrated by an event that Elisha shared with one of his ministers. When the king of Aram sent an army to capture Elisha and during the night surrounded the city of Dothan where he was staying, the following happened.

When the minister of the man of God woke up early and went outside, he saw an army that had surrounded the city with horses and chariots. Elisha's minister said to him, "Look my master! What shall we do?" Elisha answered, "Fear not! They who are with us are more than those who are with them." Elisha prayed to the Lord, "Open his eyes that he may see." The Lord opened the eyes of the young man and he saw that the mountain was full of horses and chariots of fire around Elisha. 2 Kings 6:15-17

The Scripture also teaches:

You are God's children who have overcome false prophets because greater is He Who is in you than he who is in the world. 1 John 4:3

When we respond to God's calling to fulfill our purposes in life, we are not afraid of threatening circumstances. Like Moses, Elisha, and others we realize that the power of the God is with us. This moves us to seek and find the roles that have been ordained for us regardless of the circumstances.

• **Seeking and Finding**

Two elements of trust in God are related to this Principle of Belief and Practice of Faith with reference to waiting. They are *seeking* and *finding*.

Seeking

Moses came to recognize the purpose of his life by seeking out the Hebrew people. Was that what his parents intended when they put him in a basket on the river? Did they expect him to become a leader of the Hebrew people? Is it what the Scripture meant when it declared that Moses' parents saw that he was an "unusual" child? Essentially, God frequently reveals to others His calling for us long before we are *aware* of it or even before we are *grown*.

Often, for us to find our purpose in life we have to seek God for directions. This might lead us to uncomfortable circumstances, but God will reveal to us what we should do even if we make mistakes along the way.

In the passage of Scripture below Jesus teaches about *seeking*. This same passage support what I state below regarding *finding*.

> *I tell you, "Ask, and it shall be given you; seek, and you shall find; knock, and it shall be opened to you. For everyone who asks he or she receives; and the person who seeks finds; and for the person who knocks it shall be opened. If a child shall ask bread of any of you who is a father or mother, will you give him or her a stone? Or, if he or she shall ask for a fish, will you for a fish give him or her a serpent? Or,*

if he or she shall ask for an egg, will you give him or her a scorpion? If you then being human know how to give good gifts to your children, how much more shall your heavenly Father give the Holy Spirit to them who ask Him?"
Luke 11:9-13

<u>Finding</u>
The author of the Book of Hebrews interpretation of the Exodus 2:15 in Hebrews 11:27 is that Moses' flight from Egypt was a spiritual experience. For this reason, I conclude that Moses was running away because he was afraid that if he did not escape he would not fulfill his purpose in life.

Exodus 2:15

When Pharaoh heard this thing, he sought to kill Moses. But, Moses fled from the face of Pharaoh, and dwelled in the land of Midian…

Hebrews 11: 27

> *By faith Moses left Egypt, not fearing the anger of Pharaoh. He endured as though he saw the Person Who is invisible.*

Additionally, the writer of the Book of Acts interpretation of Moses' flight from Egypt supports my impression that Moses left Egypt because he was concerned about fulfilling a leadership role with the Hebrew people after he killed the Egyptian.

Acts 7:27-29

> *The man who was attacking his Hebrew brother pushed Moses away, saying, "Who made you a ruler and a judge over us? Will you kill me as you did the Egyptian yesterday?" Then Moses fled because of what was said. He became a stranger in the land of Midian.*

• **Waiting and Typology**

Largely, the in the meanwhile of belief and faith is tied to *waiting*. There were several "in the meanwhiles" of Moses' belief and faith during his life. Those "in the meanwhiles" of belief and faith served Moses as times for his preparation for ministry and leadership.

There are at least three typologies of Moses' preparation for leadership and ministry. They are typologies in that Moses is an example for us in terms of preparing for leadership and ministry.

1. Moses was prepared for leadership for three months through the nurturing of his mother.

> *When Moses was born, he was an exceedingly special child in the sight of God.* ***He was nourished in his parents' home for three months****. When he was put outside, Pharaoh's*

403

daughter took him and nourished him as her own son. Acts 7:20-21

2. Moses was prepared for leadership for forty years by formal education and the experience of being royalty in Pharaoh's courts.

> ***Moses was taught all the wisdom of the Egyptians.*** *He was mighty in words and in deeds.* ***When he was forty years old,*** *it came into his heart to visit his people, the children of Israel. Acts 7:22-23*

3. Moses was prepared for leadership and ministry for forty years in the deserts of Midian. He eventually led the Israelites through the Sinai Peninsula desert for forty years.

> *Then Moses fled because of what was said.* ***He became a nomad in the land of Midian,*** *where he had two sons.* ***After forty years,*** *an angel of God appeared to him in a flame of fire*

Waiting

in a bush in the wilderness of Mount Sinai. Acts 7:29-30

God prepares us for leadership and ministry through processes. This followship at times requires us to wait on Him. As I previously stated, an important element of trusting God is waiting on Him. Moses, in spite his seemingly hot temper, had good intentions. All the same, he was not ready for the task that would demand much patience on his part to lead hundreds of thousands of people through the desert to the Promised Land. Correspondingly, we are from time to time not ready for what God calls us to do. But if we wait, He will prepare us for the leadership and the ministry to do His will.

Rhema and Reciprocity (A Volume of 12 Cassettes Tapes or CDs)

Glory! (A Volume of 24 Cassettes or CDs and Study Manual)

"I Am" (A Volume of 16 Cassettes or CDs)

Prophecy, Prayer, and Promise (A Set of 5 CDs or DVDs)

Spirituality: Living Victoriously! (A Volume of 36 Cassettes Tapes and Study Manual)

Common Sense for Living: 36 Lessons from the Book of Proverbs (A Volume of 36 Cassettes or CDs)

Relations, Relatives, and Relationships (2006 year long series of cassettes and video tapes or DVDs)

Books by Dr. Beresford Adams Soon to be Released

Principles of Belief and Practices of Faith: A Guide to Successful Living, Part 4

Principles of Belief and Practices of Faith: A Guide to Successful Living, Volume II

Common Sense for Living: Wise Sayings in Other Words, 36 Lessons from the Book of Proverbs

Managing Faith Crises as Opportunities (March 2009)

History, Herstory, and Ourstory (May 2009) [Textbook] Glory! (April 2009) [*Available also in Spanish*]

"I Am"

Rhema and Reciprocity (July 2009)

A Psalm to Remember: Studies from the Book of Psalms [*Available also in Spanish*] (Sept. 2009)

Belief Matters and Faith Works

Principles of Belief and Practices of Faith:
A Guide to Successful Living, Part 5
Principles of Belief and Practices of Faith:
A Guide to Successful Living, Part 6
Principles of Belief and Practices of Faith:
A Guide to Successful Living, Volume 2
"I Am" [Annotated with Hebrew, Aramaic,
Ugaritic, and Greek]
Principles of Belief and Practices of Faith:
A Guide to Successful Living, Part 7
Principles of Belief and Practices of Faith:
A Guide to Successful Living, Part 8
Principles of Belief and Practices of Faith:
A Guide to Successful Living, Part 9
Principles of Belief and Practices of Faith:
A Guide to Successful Living, Volume 3
Belief Matters and Faith Works
δοχα (Praise!)
Goodness, Grace, Mercy

```
┌─────────────────────────────────────────────┐
│      Audio book by Dr. Beresford Adams        │
│            Soon to be Released                │
└─────────────────────────────────────────────┘
```

"I Am"

```
┌─────────────────────────────────────────────┐
│      Workbooks by Dr. Beresford Adams         │
│            Soon to be Released                │
└─────────────────────────────────────────────┘
```

Principles of Belief and Practices of Faith: A Guide to Successful Living, Volume I (Dec. 2009)
Principles of Belief and Practices of Faith: A Guide to Successful Living, Volume 2
Principles of Belief and Practices of Faith: A Guide to Successful Living, Volume 3

```
┌─────────────────────────────────────────────┐
│      Devotional Booklets by Dr. Beresford     │
│         Adams Soon to be Released             │
└─────────────────────────────────────────────┘
```

Common Sense for Living: Lessons from the Book of Proverbs (May 2009)
You Are More Than You Are! (Oct. 2009)
Spirituality: Living Victoriously! [Devotional and Journal]

```
┌─────────────────────────────────────────────┐
│       Journal by Dr. Beresford Adams          │
│            Soon to be Released                │
└─────────────────────────────────────────────┘
```

Belief Matters and Faith Works

!Gloria!
Estudios desde el Libro de Salmos

So What?
Inspirational Sayings and More
The Power of Paradox
The Tao of Followership
7 Habits for Effective Prayers (Oct. 2008)

Spirituality: Living Victoriously (Sept. 2009) (This journal includes inspirational thoughts by Dr. Gloria E. Adams)

Principle, Practice, and Prosperity

A Center for Spirituality

Dr. Beresford Adams

Dr. Gloria Elena Adams

www.beeandgeepublishers.com

411

Belief Matters and Faith Works

An Institute for Spiritual Learning

Dr. Beresford Adams
Dr. Gloria Elena Adams

www.beeandgeepublishers.com

412

Bee and Gee International Ministries

Dr. Beresford Adams
Dr. Gloria Elena Adams

www.beeandgeepublishers.com

When we apply principles of belief to life situations, they become practices of faith. **Practices of faith are about being practical and pragmatic as opposed to just being theoretical.** *Merely believing in something doesn't make it happen necessarily all by itself.*

Bee and Gee Publishers
Coram, NY
www.beeandgeepublishers.com

ISBN 0-9725275-3-2

2346493